BAKE IT,
don't fake it!

BAKE IT,
don't fake it!

A Pastry Chef
Shares Her Secrets
for Impressive
(and Easy)
From-Scratch
Desserts

HEATHER BERTINETTI
FOREWORD BY RACHAEL RAY

RACHAEL RAY BOOKS
—
ATRIA

NEW YORK   LONDON   TORONTO   SYDNEY   NEW DELHI

ATRIA BOOKS

A Division of Simon & Schuster, Inc.
1230 Avenue of the Americas
New York, NY 10020

First Rachael Ray Books / Atria Books hardcover edition November 2013

RACHAEL RAY BOOKS / **ATRIA** BOOKS and colophon are trademarks of Simon & Schuster, Inc.

For information about special discounts for bulk purchases, please contact Simon & Schuster Special Sales at 1-866-506-1949 or business@simonandschuster.com.

The Simon & Schuster Speakers Bureau can bring authors to your live event. For more information, or to book an event, contact the Simon & Schuster Speakers Bureau at 1-866-248-3049 or visit our website at www.simonspeakers.com.

Manufactured in China

10 9 8 7 6 5 4 3 2 1

Library of Congress Cataloging-in-Publication Data

Bertinetti, Heather.
  Bake it, don't fake it! : a pastry chef shares her secrets for impressive (and easy) from-scratch desserts / Heather Bertinetti ; foreword by Rachael Ray.
     pages cm
1. Desserts. 2. Baking. I. Title.
  TX773.B4865 2013
  641.86—dc23
                          2013022434

ISBN 978-1-4767-3554-2
ISBN 978-1-4767-3556-6 (ebook)

This book is dedicated to the memory of my
Aunt Julie, with love.

FOREWORD BY RACHAEL RAY

I am a good cook and a terrible baker. Baking requires patience, skill, a scientific mind, precision—right? Wrong. Heather Bertinetti can make anyone and everyone a weekend pastry chef. If you wish you had the skills and confidence to make scrumptious, showstopping desserts, you've picked up the right book—*Bake It, Don't Fake It!* Heather Bertinetti is a gifted pastry chef who's honed her craft in some of New York City's top restaurants and now she's revealing her secrets for creating *to-die-for* desserts. Yes—Heather's got everything covered for rookies and seasoned bakers alike. With her help, anyone can master Banana Cream Pie to Hazelnut Dacquoise Roulade. Head to your local supermarket for easy-to-find ingredients and enjoy making your own desserts, entirely from scratch, with the ease of an expert baker. You'll impress your friends, family, and even yourself in no time! Bake it. Don't fake it.

contents

introduction

I think it's very rare to actually grow up to be what you always said you wanted to be when you were a kid.

Growing up, my favorite hobby was baking at home for my family. Blame it on my Easy-Bake Oven, but it was truly love at first bite! While most little girls my age were doodling hearts with crushes' initials in them, I was drawing plated desserts on my folders and lunch bags. I loved imagining all the different flavor and color options for cakes and frostings. I loved making edible art. And most of all I loved the reaction I got when people ate my creations. I knew at a very young age that pastry was my calling. Baking was something I was good at, and it was my go-to answer for the "what would you like to be when you grow up" essay question. I never once wrote anything different.

Fortunately I was able to pursue that passion in culinary school and to learn the reality of choosing baking as a career. Thrown into the hot seat at an early age, I was pastry chef at some of the most popular, most visible restaurants in Manhattan. It was sink or swim and I rose to the challenge. How exciting for me as a young chef to have a huge kitchen as my "office" and to be able to create, invent, and collaborate with talented partners to design dessert menus and serve the most discriminating palates!

Once I had met that challenge, though, I began to sense that I had a bigger goal. I realized that the most gratifying thing to me about being an executive pastry chef was teaching my cooks techniques and recipes, helping them hone their skills. And now that desire to teach what I know has outgrown the boundaries of the restaurant kitchen.

I feel quite passionate that I can help anyone understand baking. I really enjoy explaining the in and outs of baking, and I feel that if I can give people that knowledge, they will feel empowered to do it themselves and be inspired to create. Cooking from scratch gives you such a sense of achievement . . . and it's just plain better eats! There is really nothing that can compare with a homemade dessert. The proof is in the pudding (literally).

I feel especially compelled to prove this point because I meet so many people who tell me that they're scared of baking . . . that they "fake it" by buying pre-made desserts or using mixes. I just know that I can fix that. That's why I wrote this book. It is the next phase in my career. If I can help you understand baking, then I consider that a "mission accomplished" for me.

So that's my mission, now let's get started. Before anything else, go to "Read Me First!" (page 11). This is where I give you the important information about how to use this book—what ingredients and equipment I use, and how I use them. And how to measure ingredients!

From there you can move on to the first chapter, which I've called "Baking 101." Here are the basic techniques and recipes that will help you gain a good understanding of baking, as well as tips that will steer you clear of mistakes (my whipped cream looks like butter . . . now what?). This chapter is one of my favorites because it is your foundation for everything else. But even a basic recipe can get dressed up and be something special, so throughout the chapter I've included Chef It Up! tips where I will tell you what I would do with the cake or pie or cookie if I were serving it in one of my restaurants.

Following the basics in "Baking 101" is a chapter called "Beyond Baking." In a restaurant, the pastry chef is usually in charge of the entire dessert menu, which is a whole lot more than baked goods. So this chapter will introduce you to basic desserts like custards, sorbets, crêpes, poached fruit, simple candies, and more.

Once you've mastered all the basics, you can move on to the somewhat more demanding recipes in the chapter called "The Next Level." These recipes are not necessarily more difficult to accomplish, but they can demand more of your time and may call for specialized pieces of cooking equipment (like a pizzelle iron). As with the "Baking 101" recipes, these recipes may also get Chef It Up! tips so you can really impress people with your dessert skills.

At this point, you're a pro, ready to take on the world—and maybe a couple of serious challenges. So for the super ambitious, I end with a chapter called "Showstoppers." The St. Honoré Cake (page 173) is a prime example. Although it is a labor-intensive cake, you will be able to make it easily, with all your knowledge from the previous chapters. This is truly a special-occasion cake.

My hope is that if you bake your way through this book, you'll be putting desserts on the table that might even fool your guests into thinking that you secretly went to culinary school.

—Heather Bertinetti
November 2013

P.S. Check out my blog: "Bake It, Don't Fake It!" at hbertinetti.com

read me first!

MEASURING

In a professional pastry kitchen, all ingredients are measured by weighing them on a scale—even water! It's the only sure way to guarantee the ratios of fat to flour or liquid to dry that will give you the results you want. However, the recipes in this book have been written with volume measurements instead, because they are more user friendly for the home cook. There is one key technique that is absolutely critical to the success of your baked goods when you're not using a scale. And that is *how* you measure ingredients, especially dry ingredients like flour and sugar.

TO MEASURE LIQUID INGREDIENTS, use a glass or other see-through measuring cup. Put the cup on a level surface and crouch down until your eye is level with the markings on the cup.

TO MEASURE DRY INGREDIENTS, such as flour, sugar, cocoa powder, and cornstarch, use what are called "dry measures." Those are the graduated cups (usually nesting) that have handles and look like little saucepans. Here's how you do it:

1. Place the size of dry measure you need on a sheet of wax paper.

2. Lightly spoon the ingredient out of the storage container into the cup, letting it pile higher than the rim of the cup.

3. Take the straight side of a table knife and sweep it across the rim to level off the excess. Use the wax paper to return the excess to the storage container.

INGREDIENTS

Before you begin any of the recipes in this book, it's best to know what I used when I created them. It's your surest way of achieving the right results. With a few very rare exceptions, all the ingredients in this book are available in supermarkets. Here are some notes on the very basics. For more in-depth info and some suggestions for substitutions, see the "Ingredients & Substitutions" section in the Appendix (page 190).

BUTTER: All the butter in this book is unsalted. If you only have salted butter on hand, you can use it, but omit the salt in the recipe.

EGGS: All recipes were developed with large eggs. This goes for when egg yolks or egg whites are called for, too.

MILK: When whole milk is specifically called for, do not substitute a lower fat milk; the results will suffer.

FLOUR: All flour is all-purpose unless otherwise specified, and it doesn't matter if it's bleached or unbleached.

SUGAR: This is granulated white, unless otherwise specified

SALT: All salt is kosher salt unless otherwise specified. Note that I use Diamond Crystal kosher salt. This is important, because cup for cup, Diamond Crystal is less salty than other brands of kosher salt.

CHOCOLATE: Almost all of the chocolate called for in the book is in the form of chocolate chips. It's a lot simpler to measure and deal with in the home kitchen. Supermarket brands are fine, or if you're feeling fancy, you can buy the more expensive high-end chips.

EQUIPMENT

Apart from the obvious things like bowls, wooden spoons, and rubber or silicone spatulas, here is a list of the basic pieces of equipment you need for most of the recipes in this book. In cases where more specialized equipment is needed, the individual recipes will alert you. You can read more about the equipment in the Appendix (page 197).

STAND MIXER (with paddle, whisk, and dough hook attachments)

FOOD PROCESSOR

BLENDER, stand and/or hand blender

BAKING SHEETS (at least two, if possible), 14 x 18 inches

RIMMED BAKING SHEET(S), 10 x 15 inches

CAKE PANS (at least two), 9-inch diameter, 2 inches deep

SPRINGFORM PANS, 9- and 10-inch diameter

BAKING PANS, 8-inch square and 9 x 13 inches

PIE PLATE, 9-inch

MUFFINS TIN, standard 12-cup

WIRE WHISK

ROLLING PIN

WIRE COOLING RACKS

OFFSET SPATULAS: a small one for decorating and a large one for sliding under cake layers to move them

MICROPLANE ZESTER

FINE-MESH SIEVE

PARCHMENT PAPER (very important)

NONSTICK SILICONE LINERS: These aren't required, because you can use parchment paper, but they're definitely useful. Buy a size that fits your baking sheets without leaving much surface uncovered.

Baking 101

This chapter includes a collection of basic cakes, cookies, pies, and pastries. They're for beginning bakers, but also for veterans who want to hone their skills. You'll find yourself making these time and time again, as they are the foundations for both everyday and restaurant-worthy desserts.

Basic Yellow Cake (page 16)
with Swiss Buttercream (page 70)

BASIC YELLOW CAKE

MAKES TWO 9-INCH LAYERS

Everyone needs a good go-to yellow cake recipe in their recipe file. Yellow cake has become the most common birthday cake flavor. Its neutral flavor profile allows the cake to be dressed up with any filling and frosting from chocolate to fruit. This recipe is moist, buttery, and perfectly simple.

Cooking spray
3½ cups cake flour
1 tablespoon baking powder
1 teaspoon baking soda
1 teaspoon kosher salt
1 cup buttermilk
½ cup sour cream

3 tablespoons vegetable oil
½ pound (2 sticks) unsalted butter, at
    room temperature
2 cups sugar
5 large eggs
3 large egg yolks
1 tablespoon vanilla extract

Preheat the oven to 350°F. Line the bottoms of two 9 x 2-inch cake pans with parchment paper rounds. Coat the pan and paper with cooking spray.

In a medium bowl, whisk together the flour, baking powder, baking soda, and salt. In a separate bowl, whisk the buttermilk, sour cream, and oil.

In a stand mixer fitted with the paddle attachment, cream the butter and sugar on medium speed until light and fluffy. Reduce the speed to low, add the whole eggs one at time, beating well after each addition. Beat in the egg yolks and vanilla until incorporated. On medium speed, alternate adding the flour mixture and the buttermilk mixture to the batter in several additions, ending with the buttermilk mixture. Scrape down the bowl with a rubber spatula and beat until the batter is blended well.

Scrape the batter into the prepared pans and place both pans on the same oven rack. Bake until the cake springs back to the touch and a cake tester inserted in the center comes out clean, 30 to 40 minutes; rotate the pans from front to back halfway through.

Let the cakes cool completely in the pans before filling and frosting.

chef it up!

Coconut Cake: Spread the bottom layer with Coconut Custard (page 92) and top with the second layer. Frost the top and sides with Swiss Buttercream (page 70). Lightly toast shredded coconut in the oven and cover the cake (top and sides) with the toasted coconut.

Strawberry "Shortcake": Spread the bottom layer with a thin layer of raspberry jam. Top with Whipped Cream (page 80). Top with ½ cup sliced strawberries, keeping them toward the center (you don't want them poking out when you put the top layer on). Put the top layer on and frost the top and sides with more whipped cream. Shave white chocolate curls on top.

INSIDER TIP • DRIES AND WETS

Many batters start out with a base of butter, sugar, and eggs to which are then added the dry ingredients and the wet ingredients. Typically the "dries" (flour, baking powder, baking soda, cocoa powder, etc.) are mixed together in a separate bowl. And the "wets" (milk, juice, oil, flavorings, or other liquids) are mixed together in yet another bowl. The dries and wets are then added alternately to the creamed butter and sugar. The reason for alternating their addition is to make a smooth batter. If you were to add all the wets first, followed by the all the dries, the batter would not be homogeneous; the fat would be separated out and the resulting cake would be greasy and flat.

BASIC CHOCOLATE CAKE

MAKES TWO 9-INCH LAYERS

This basic chocolate cake is what is called a "high-ratio cake," meaning it contains a large amount of sugar and fat (butter and/or oil)—compared to lower-fat cakes like sponge cakes—which makes it extremely moist. Because high-ratio cakes are so moist, they are too heavy to use for multitiered cakes—like wedding cakes—and instead are used to make only two or three layers. (Typically, a wedding cake would be a lighter cake, such as a sponge cake.) The addition of coffee is a common technique used to both deepen the flavor of the chocolate and add moisture.

Cooking spray
4 tablespoons (½ stick) unsalted
   butter, at room temperature
2 cups sugar
2 large eggs
2 tablespoons vanilla extract
1¾ cups + 1 tablespoon all-purpose flour
1 cup unsweetened cocoa powder, sifted

1½ teaspoons baking soda
½ teaspoon + a pinch of baking powder
¾ teaspoon kosher salt
1 cup hot brewed coffee
½ cup + 1 tablespoon buttermilk
½ cup + 1 tablespoon canola oil
½ cup sour cream

Preheat the oven to 350°F. Line the bottoms of two 9 x 2-inch round cake pans with parchment paper rounds. Coat the pans and paper with cooking spray.

In a stand mixer fitted with the paddle attachment, cream the butter and sugar on medium speed until light and fluffy. Reduce the speed to low and add the eggs one at a time, beating well after each addition. Beat in the vanilla.

In a medium bowl, whisk together the flour, cocoa, baking soda, baking powder, and salt. In a separate bowl, whisk together the coffee, buttermilk, oil, and sour cream. On medium speed, alternate adding the flour mixture and the buttermilk mixture to the butter-egg mixture in several additions, mixing until everything is combined. Scrape down the bowl with a rubber spatula and beat until the batter is blended well.

Scrape the batter into the prepared pans and place both on the same oven rack. Bake until the cake springs back to the touch and a cake tester comes out clean, 20 to 35 minutes; rotate the pans from front to back halfway through. Let the cakes cool completely in the pans before filling and frosting.

chef it up!

Chocolate Raspberry Cake: Stir ¼ cup raspberry jam into ½ cup Vanilla Pastry Cream (page 77) and spread that over the bottom layer. Top with fresh raspberries. Top with the second layer and frost the top and sides with Ganache Filling (page 75). Decorate the top with more fresh raspberries.

Chocolate Hazelnut Cake: See page 160.

INSIDER TIP • CREAMING BUTTER AND SUGAR

If you've done any baking at all, you've probably seen the instruction "cream the butter and sugar until light and fluffy." But did you know that you can take it too far? If you go beyond the "fluffy" stage (the mixture will look curdled), the butter will have gotten too warm, releasing the air bubbles that you beat into it. The result? A flat cake or cookie.

BROWNIES

MAKES ONE 9 X 13-INCH PAN

Brownies are so simple to make at home, I have never understood why anyone would ever use the boxed kind. For the richest brownies, the ratio of chocolate to butter (by weight) is always 1:1. These are pure decadence.

Cooking spray
1 pound semisweet chocolate chips
  (about 2⅔ cups)
1 pound (4 sticks) unsalted butter
7 large eggs

1 teaspoon vanilla extract
3½ cups sugar
¾ cup + 1 tablespoon all-purpose flour
⅓ cup unsweetened cocoa powder,
  sifted

Preheat the oven to 350°F. Coat a 9 x 13-inch baking pan with cooking spray.

In a large heatproof bowl set over a pot of simmering water, melt the chocolate and butter. Take the bowl off the pot and quickly whisk in the eggs until the batter is homogeneous. Whisk in the vanilla, then the sugar, flour, and cocoa.

Scrape the batter into the prepared pan and bake until a cake tester comes out clean, 25 to 30 minutes; rotate the pan from front to back halfway through.

Let the brownies cool in the pan before cutting into squares or bars. Store in an airtight container for up to 1 week.

chef it up! BROWNIE FLUFF-A-NUTTER

Bake the brownie and cool it in the pan. Place in the freezer for 2 to 3 hours (this keeps it intact when you take it out of the pan). Invert the brownie out of the pan and turn right-side up. With a serrated knife, trim the top "crust" off the brownie, making it flat and even. Spread with ¼ inch Peanut Butter Filling (½ recipe; page 76); top that with 1½ cups Chocolate Glaze (½ recipe; page 66). Let cool and set for about 1 hour. To serve, make a generous smear of Marshmallow Creme (page 121) across a plate; toast with a blow-torch (aka a crème brûlée torch). Cut the brownie into thin bars and place on the fluff. Top with crushed candied peanuts (see "Candied Nuts," page 46).

ORANGE BUTTERMILK BUNDT CAKE

SERVES 16

A Bundt cake is essentially a pound cake, which has a very fine texture, making it especially well suited to keeping a shape, like that of a Bundt pan. (Of course it can also be baked in a loaf or plain tube pan, like a traditional pound cake.) Pound cakes are often used as the layers in ice cream cakes, or in the British dessert called trifle, or in my Cake Pudding (page 94). This pound cake is a great basic citrus cake recipe. The buttermilk not only adds moistness but also gives the cake a slight extra tang. The orange can be interchanged with other types of citrus, such as lemon or grapefruit. With its light and yummy fruit flavor, this cake is perfect after a heavy meal. **SPECIAL EQUIPMENT:** 12-cup Bundt pan

Cooking spray and flour, for prepping the pan
½ pound + ⅓ cup (2⅔ sticks) unsalted butter, at room temperature
2¾ cups sugar
6 large eggs
4 large egg yolks
¾ cup buttermilk

2 tablespoons grapeseed or canola oil
1½ teaspoons grated orange zest
1½ tablespoons orange juice
1½ teaspoons vanilla extract
3¾ cups all-purpose flour
1 tablespoon baking powder
Pinch of kosher salt
White Glaze (page 65)

Preheat the oven to 325°F. Coat a 12-cup Bundt pan with cooking spray, then lightly coat with flour, shaking out the excess.

In a stand mixer fitted with the paddle attachment, cream the butter and sugar on medium speed until light and fluffy. Reduce to low speed and add the whole eggs and egg yolks one at a time, beating well after each addition.

In a medium bowl, whisk together the buttermilk, oil, orange zest and juice, and vanilla. In a second bowl, stir together the flour, baking powder, and salt.

On medium speed, alternate adding the flour mixture and the buttermilk mixture to the butter-egg mixture in several additions, ending with the flour mixture. Scrape down the bowl with a rubber spatula and beat until the batter is blended well.

Scrape the batter into the prepared pan. Bake the cake until a cake tester inserted halfway between the center tube and outside of the pan comes out clean, 50 minutes to 1 hour; rotate the pan front to back halfway through. Let the cake cool in the pan.

While the cake is cooling, make the glaze.

Set a wire cooling rack over a piece of parchment paper (for easy cleanup). Invert the cooled cake out of the pan onto the rack. Pour the glaze over the cake, letting it drip down the sides.

chef it up!

I sometimes bake this cake in 4-ounce brown paper baking cups (they're like freestanding muffin cups, waxed on the inside and sturdy). For a touch of added sweetness and visual appeal, I sprinkle a little pearlized sugar on top before baking. Each "cup" cake then gets a little ribbon wrapped around it for a cute takeaway gift.

INSIDER TIP • STORING BUNDT CAKES

These dense buttery cakes store really well. Keep them in an airtight container at room temperature for up to 2 weeks. It's important to keep them well covered to prevent drying out.

ANGEL FOOD CAKE

SERVES 16

Angel food cake is an egg white–based cake that is so simple to mix, it makes for a great quick and easy dessert. With its light-as-air texture and spongy crumb, this cake is a good one to sauce or soak up fruit juices released from macerated berries. It's the cake you make for a non-gut-busting meal on a warm summer's night. **SPECIAL EQUIPMENT:** 9-inch tube pan with removable bottom (aka angel food cake pan)

1½ cups confectioners' sugar
1 cup cake flour
12 large egg whites, at room
   temperature
½ teaspoon kosher salt

1 teaspoon cream of tartar
1 teaspoon vanilla extract
Lemon Glaze (page 65)
Fresh berries, for garnish

Preheat the oven to 350°F.

Sift 1 cup of the confectioners' sugar with the cake flour two times and set aside. Sift the remaining ½ cup confectioners' sugar separately and set aside.

In a stand mixer fitted with the whisk attachment, beat the egg whites with the salt and cream of tartar on high speed. When the whites have reached the soft peak stage, add the sifted ½ cup sugar and the vanilla. Continue to whip the whites to stiff peaks. With a rubber spatula, gently fold in the flour mixture until combined and fully incorporated.

Pour the batter into the tube pan. Bake until light golden brown and a cake tester comes out clean, 35 to 45 minutes; rotate the pan front to back halfway through.

An angel food cake needs to be cooled upside down to keep it light and airy (otherwise gravity causes it to sink into itself). Some tube pans come with little feet that will support the tube pan when it's upside down. If the pan you're using doesn't have little feet, invert the pan and hang it by the center tube on a narrow-necked bottle. Let cool completely.

While the cake is cooling, make the glaze.

Release the cake from the pan by running a knife around the edges, then popping off the side walls. Set a wire cooling rack over a piece of parchment paper (for easy cleanup). Invert the cooled cake out of the pan onto the rack. Pour the glaze over the cake, letting it drip down the sides.

To serve, cut the cake with a serrated knife. Serve with fresh berries alongside, or for a fancier presentation, see "Chef It Up!" below.

chef it up!

Instead of plain fresh berries, macerate them first, meaning let them sit with sugar to develop juices. Then when you serve the cake, you top slices with berries and also spoon some of the juices over the top. To make the berries, combine 1 pint berries (your choice) with ½ cup sugar, stir and let sit for at least 1 hour at room temperature, until the sugar pulls some of the juices out of the fruit.

INSIDER TIP • ANGEL FOOD CAKE PANS

Because angel food cake batter is some sticky, temperamental stuff, it's important to use a cake pan with a removable bottom for an easy release of the cake. Don't spray or grease the pan, because you want the meringue-style batter to climb the walls of the pan. If the pan were greased, the batter would have nothing to cling to and it would collapse and be dense.

HAZELNUT DACQUOISE ROULADE

SERVES 10 TO 12

Adacquoise is a French-style layer cake made with layers of a baked nut-based meringue and a filling, often buttercream (see "Buttercreams," page 68). One of the first desserts I ever put on a restaurant menu as a pastry chef was an elaborate cake based on the same idea, though its inspiration was Italian. It was layers of the hazelnut meringue in this recipe filled with a semifreddo. The nut meringue makes a very sturdy—and flexible—cake layer that is made here into a roulade, filled and rolled like a jelly roll. A simple but really impressive way to wow your family and friends. **SPECIAL EQUIPMENT:** cake comb (optional)

1¼ cups large egg whites (about 7 large eggs)
6 tablespoons granulated sugar
1¼ cups confectioners' sugar

1½ cup blanched hazelnuts, finely ground (see "Nut Flours," page 29)
Mocha Ganache (page 75)

Preheat the oven to 325°F. Line an 11 x 17-inch rimmed baking sheet with parchment paper or a nonstick silicone liner.

In a stand mixer fitted with the whisk attachment, beat the egg whites on high speed while slowly adding the granulated sugar until stiff peaks form. Transfer the whites to a separate, larger bowl and using a rubber spatula, gently fold in the confectioners' sugar and ground hazelnuts until combined.

Spread the batter out on the lined pan. Bake the cake for 10 minutes, then rotate the pan front to back. Bake until the cake looks light brown and dry on top and forms a slight crust, about 10 minutes longer. Let the cake cool completely in the pan.

Run a small knife around the edges of the cake and pan to help release it. Turn the cake out, top down, onto a flat surface lined with a larger piece of

(continued on page 29)

parchment paper. Spoon about 2 cups of ganache in the center of the cake and with an offset spatula, spread it over the cake, leaving a ½-inch border all around. Lift up the parchment paper on one of the short sides and roll the cake onto itself. When you reach the end, roll the cake so that it sits seam side down. Frost the outside of the cake with the remaining ganache. (If you have a cake comb, run it down the length of the ganache to give the cake a ridged texture.) Chill the cake for about 1 hour to set the ganache.

Let the cake come to room temperature before serving. Dip a knife in very hot water to heat it, then dry it off and trim both ends off the roulade to make a prettier presentation. Cut the roulade crosswise into slices to serve.

chef it up!

This is already a pretty impressive-looking dessert, but for some serious wow, this is how I would present it: Cut the roulade slices on a slight angle instead of straight down. Plate the slice on a swoosh of Chocolate Sauce (page 82). Sprinkle with some candied hazelnuts (see "Candied Nuts," page 46) and serve with a scoop of Espresso Ice Cream (page 109).

INSIDER TIP • NUT FLOURS

Although you can buy some nut flours, you're much better off making your own because the oils in ground nuts can easily go rancid. (In fact, if you do buy nut flours, be sure to keep them in the freezer.) To grind nuts, use a food processor and grind them in pulses until they are fine-textured. Do not overprocess or process too quickly or you'll end up with nut butter instead of nut flour.

PLAIN CHEESECAKE

SERVES 8 TO 12

The crust here is the classic graham cracker crust, but any cookie can be used to take the cheesecake in a slightly different direction. Try chocolate wafer cookies, shortbread, vanilla wafers, or gingersnaps. As for the batter itself, I like to use a mix of both heavy cream and sour cream to give the cake a more creamy consistency. When baked, sour cream sets harder than straight heavy cream, so the cream is necessary for the smooth soft texture.

GRAHAM CRACKER CRUST
Cooking spray
2 cups graham cracker crumbs
   (preferably Teddy Grahams)
½ cup confectioners' sugar
½ teaspoon kosher salt
¼ pound (1 stick) unsalted butter,
   melted
1 teaspoon vanilla extract

BATTER
4 packages (8 ounces each) cream
   cheese, at room temperature
1½ cups granulated sugar
1 teaspoon kosher salt
5 large eggs, at room temperature
¾ cup crème fraîche or sour cream, at
   room temperature
¼ cup heavy cream, at room
   temperature
1 tablespoon vanilla extract

MAKE THE CRUST: Preheat the oven to 325°F. Line the bottom of a 10-inch springform pan with a parchment paper round and coat the paper with cooking spray. Wrap the outside of the pan with foil, just at the bottom where the seam is. (The pan is going into a water bath and you don't want any water to get in.)

In a bowl, stir together the crumbs, confectioners' sugar, and salt. Add the butter and vanilla and mix until blended well. Press the crumb mixture onto the bottom and 1 inch up the sides of the pan. Bake for 10 minutes to set the crust. Take the crust out of the oven and set aside to cool completely. Leave the oven on.

MAKE THE FILLING: In a stand mixer fitted with the paddle attachment, beat the cream cheese, granulated sugar, and salt on medium speed until creamy, about 2 minutes. Reduce to low speed and beat in the eggs one at a time. Beat in the crème fraîche, heavy cream, and vanilla. Scrape down the bowl with a rubber spatula and beat on medium speed until the filling is blended well but not aerated.

Choose a roasting pan that will hold the springform pan. Place the roasting pan on a pulled-out rack in the oven and place the springform pan in the center of the roasting pan. Pour the batter into the springform, then pour hot water into the roasting pan (staying well away from the springform, so you don't get any water into the cheesecake batter) to come halfway up the sides of the springform pan. Gently slide the rack back into place and close the oven door.

Bake until the center slightly jiggles, about 1 hour 20 minutes. Turn off the oven and leave the cheesecake inside to completely cool, about 6 hours. Take it out of the water bath, cover, and refrigerate for at least 4 hours or overnight.

Remove the pan sides and cut into slices.

chef it up!

When I make a cheesecake for a restaurant, I freeze it after it's been chilled. There are two reasons for this. One is that I always remove the cheesecake from the bottom of the springform pan because it makes a nicer presentation, and the best way to do that without a disaster is to freeze the cheesecake first. Also, a frozen cheesecake gives you much cleaner slices. When I serve a slice of this, I like to top it with Cinnamon Whipped Cream (page 80).

INSIDER TIP • NO-CRACK CHEESECAKES

Cheesecakes are delicious no matter what they look like, but if you want to bake one like a pro, then you have to take some steps to be sure that the top doesn't crack as it bakes. Here's what you have to do to avoid that: First, always make sure your ingredients are at room temperature. If the mixture is cold, then the cake will crack when it hits the hot oven. Always bake the cake in a water bath, which will create gentle, even heat for cooking the custard-based batter, and then allow the cake to cool completely in the water bath in a turned-off oven.

DULCE DE LECHE POWDER PUFF COOKIES

MAKES 24 COOKIES

I am a lover of Latin cuisine, so much so that one of my favorite flavors to work with is dulce de leche. This delicately sweet cookie is reminiscent of a shortbread cookie because of its buttery, crumbly texture. It serves as a perfect end to a meal, accompanied with some café con leche.

½ pound (2 sticks) cold unsalted
  butter, cubed
¾ cup confectioners' sugar, plus more
  for dusting
2 cups all-purpose flour

1 teaspoon vanilla extract
Pinch of kosher salt
2½ tablespoons dulce de leche
  (available at most supermarkets)

Preheat the oven to 350°F. Line a baking sheet with parchment paper (see "Batch Baking," page 137).

Using a food processer fitted with the plastic blade, combine the butter and ¾ cup confectioners' sugar and pulse until the mixture has a pebbly texture. Add the flour, vanilla, salt, and dulce de leche. Continue to process the mixture until a dough forms.

Scoop out the dough by tablespoons and roll into balls. Space the balls 1½ to 2 inches apart on the baking sheet. Bake until golden brown, about 10 minutes; rotate the pan front to back halfway through.

Transfer the cookies to wire racks to cool. Dust the cooled cookies with confectioners' sugar. Store the cookies in an airtight container at room temperature for up to 1 week.

OATMEAL RAISIN COOKIES

MAKES 16 COOKIES

These cookies are deliciously chewy with a hint of cinnamon to bring it all together. Great by themselves, of course, but think about using them for an ice cream sandwich for a fun twist on a classic!

6 ounces (1½ sticks) unsalted butter, melted
2 tablespoons light corn syrup
1 cup packed dark brown sugar
½ cup granulated sugar
1 large egg
1 large egg yolk
½ teaspoon vanilla extract

1 teaspoon ground cinnamon
2 cups + 2 tablespoons all-purpose flour
1 cup + 2 tablespoons quick-cooking oats
½ teaspoon baking soda
½ teaspoon kosher salt
1 cup raisins (combo of light and dark)

Preheat the oven to 325°F. Line a baking sheet with parchment paper.

In a stand mixer fitted with the paddle attachment, beat together the butter, corn syrup, brown sugar, and granulated sugar on medium speed. On low speed, beat in the eggs one at a time. Beat in the vanilla and cinnamon. Add the flour, oats, baking soda, and salt and mix to form a dough. Fold in the raisins, just barely incorporating them into the dough. It's a very stiff dough.

With a 2-ounce (¼-cup) cookie scoop, place the dough 2 inches apart on the baking sheet. Bake until just starting to brown at the edges, 8 to 10 minutes; rotate the pan front to back halfway through. Transfer to a wire rack to cool.

INSIDER TIP • CARRYOVER BAKING

Cookies "carryover bake." This means that they continue to bake on the cookie sheet after they are pulled from the oven because of residual heat on the baking sheet. Always pull your cookies out just when they first start to brown on the edges or 1 minute early for perfect texture. You might think the cookie is still raw, but they will set as they cool.

COCONUT SHORTBREAD

MAKES 24 COOKIES

Every year I make this recipe just as summertime hits. The buttery texture makes it a great accompaniment for creamy desserts like panna cotta or ice cream. The coconut is a fun twist on a classic cookie. You could also use the dough as a base for a tart.

Cooking spray
1 pound (4 sticks) cold unsalted butter, cubed
¾ cup confectioners' sugar
2¼ cups all-purpose flour

2½ cups unsweetened shredded coconut
½ teaspoon kosher salt
1 tablespoon dark rum
1 tablespoon vanilla extract
Granulated sugar, for sprinkling

Preheat the oven to 325°F. Lightly coat a baking sheet with cooking spray.

In a stand mixer fitted with the paddle attachment, cream the butter and confectioners' sugar on medium speed until softened. Beat in the flour, coconut, salt, rum, and vanilla until combined.

Between 2 sheets of parchment paper, roll the dough out to a rectangle ½ inch thick. Sprinkle the work surface with granulated sugar and transfer the dough to the sugar. Cut the dough into bars 1 x 2½ inches. Transfer the bars to the baking sheet. Sprinkle more granulated sugar on top. Bake for 10 minutes. Rotate the pan front to back and continue to bake until light golden brown, about 5 minutes longer. Transfer the cookies to a wire rack to cool.

chef it up!

A really easy way to fancy-up shortbread is to use a shortbread mold. The shortbread you see in the photo was made in an 11½-inch round mold with a heart design. The mold is also scored for perfect portioning of the cookies. Just press the dough into the mold with your fingertips and bake until light golden brown. There's nothing like a baking tool that does all the decorating work for you!

BANANA CREAM PIE

MAKES ONE 9-INCH PIE

I love a pie that's fast and easy, and nothing could be faster or easier than a cookie crust. Plus a banana cream pie is just one of those nostalgic pies that puts a smile on your face. The buttery shortbread crust paired with vanilla rum cream and fresh bananas is truly a match made in heaven!

CRUST
2 cups ground shortbread cookies
½ cup confectioners' sugar
¼ pound (1 stick) unsalted butter, melted
1 teaspoon vanilla extract
½ teaspoon kosher salt

FILLING AND TOPPING
Vanilla Pastry Cream (page 77)
2 tablespoons dark rum
2 large or 3 small bananas, thinly sliced
1½ cups heavy cream
½ cup confectioners' sugar
1 vanilla bean, split lengthwise, or
  1 teaspoon vanilla extract

Preheat the oven to 350°F.

MAKE THE CRUST: In a bowl, stir together the shortbread crumbs, sugar, melted butter, vanilla, and salt. Press the mixture into the bottom and up the sides of a 9-inch pie plate. Bake for 10 minutes to set the crust. Let the crust cool completely before filling.

MAKE THE FILLING: Prepare the pastry cream according to the recipe and stir in the rum when you stir in the vanilla and butter.

Once the crust has cooled, spread one-third of the pastry cream evenly over the bottom of the crust. Arrange a single layer of bananas on top of the cream. Repeat this process two more times, ending with bananas.

MAKE THE TOPPING: In a stand mixer fitted with the whisk attachment, start

(continued on page 40)

whipping the cream on low speed. When the cream just begins to gain volume, slowly add the sugar and vanilla (either scrape in the seeds from the vanilla bean or add the extract). Continue to whip on medium speed until stiff peaks form.

Spread the whipped cream on top of the pie using a small offset spatula. Chill for at least 3 hours before serving.

chef it up!

Get fancy with the whipped cream here. Fit a pastry bag with a #8 star tip, scoop the cream into the bag, and pipe rosettes (see "Decorating with Icing," page 73) all around the outside edge of the pie. Since you'll be leaving some bananas exposed, lightly brush them with some lemon juice to keep them from browning. For an added flavor twist, drizzle the top of the pie (just the bananas) with some Calvados Caramel Sauce (page 81) or Chocolate Sauce (page 82).

INSIDER TIP • VANILLA PASTE

When I'm working in a restaurant kitchen, I have access to a huge supply of vanilla beans. But when I'm at home, I count pennies just like everyone else, and vanilla beans are really expensive. (Not to mention that the overpriced vanilla beans you find in supermarkets are old and dried out.) So here's the solution I've found for myself at home: I use vanilla bean paste, which is really reasonably priced. If you want to try it, you can swap it in for the vanilla beans or extract in any of my recipes. If a recipe calls for the seeds of 1 vanilla bean, use ½ teaspoon of the paste (and 2 beans would be 1 teaspoon paste); and if the recipe calls for extract, substitute the paste in an equal amount.

SIMPLE PIE DOUGH

MAKES ENOUGH FOR TWO 9-INCH PIE CRUSTS

Pies used to be my nemesis! Early on in my career, I was entered into an apple pie contest run by a very creditable magazine. I was determined to make the most perfect looking and tasting pie. After extensive research on the American classic apple pie, I was so consumed with all the tips and tricks my head was spinning. Lard versus butter, food processer versus by hand, addition of vodka to cold water, and on and on. I made my pie and, to my dismay, only came in fifth. What I learned from the experience was that it's all about personal preference when it comes to a pie. The judges weren't looking for great dough; they wanted a contemporary take on it. Pie dough is just the vessel for the entertainment on the ship—the filling. So my dough is simple, fast, and tasty too!

2 cups all-purpose flour
2 tablespoons sugar
Pinch of kosher salt

12 tablespoons (1½ sticks) cold
   unsalted butter, cubed
½ cup cold water

Mix the flour, sugar, and salt together in a pile directly on a work surface. Next "rub" the butter into the flour mixture using your fingertips until the butter pieces are the size of peas. Make a well in the center of the flour mixture, add the water to the well, and continue mixing just until combined.

Divide the dough in half and transfer each half to a sheet of plastic wrap. Press each portion out into a disk about ½ inch thick and wrap tightly with the plastic. Refrigerate the dough until firm, at least 2 hours and up to overnight.

INSIDER TIP • SHORTENING DOUGHS

Solid vegetable shortening makes a dough that maintains its shape better than one made with butter. It's good to use if you want to make decorative cutouts with the pie dough. Just swap in the same amount of shortening for the butter.

STREUSEL-TOPPED APPLE PIE

MAKES ONE 9-INCH PIE

I feel it would be un-American of me to create a baking book without an apple pie! There is something so soul soothing about this classic American dessert. And I make it all year round. It's the one dessert where I let my rules of seasonality go out the window. This apple pie has a streusel topping, which avoids the problem of having to make a top crust. However, if you prefer a two-crust pie, see "Double-Crust Pie," opposite page.

CRUST
Flour, for rolling
½ recipe Simple Pie Dough (page 41), chilled

FILLING
6 large or 8 small apples (preferably Honeycrisp or Golden Delicious), peeled, cored, and thinly sliced
½ cup packed light brown sugar
¼ cup granulated sugar
2 teaspoons lemon juice
1 teaspoon vanilla extract

1 teaspoon ground cinnamon
½ teaspoon grated nutmeg
Pinch of kosher salt
¼ to ½ cup all-purpose flour

STREUSEL
2 cups all-purpose flour
1 cup packed light brown sugar
1 teaspoon ground cinnamon
Pinch of kosher salt
1 teaspoon vanilla extract
12 tablespoons (1½ sticks) unsalted butter, melted

MAKE THE CRUST: On a well-floured surface, start flattening and rolling out the disk of dough, turning it often to keep it round. Continue to roll the dough until ⅛ inch thick and about 12 inches in diameter. Gently roll the dough onto the rolling pin. Position the dough over a 9-inch pie plate and carefully unroll the dough into the pan. Using your hands, gently press the dough into the bottom and up the sides of the pan. Tuck the excess dough under itself all around to form a raised edge.

To make a decorative edge on the crust (called "crimping"), use the pointer finger of one hand to press into the raised edge of dough while pinching the dough on either side with the thumb and pointer finger of your other hand. Do this all around the edge of the crust to create a wavy look.

Preheat the oven to 350°F.

PREPARE THE FILLING: Place the apples in a large bowl. Add the brown sugar, granulated sugar, lemon juice, vanilla, cinnamon, nutmeg, and salt. Toss around all the ingredients using a spoon. Sprinkle ¼ cup flour over the top and mix in as well. If your apples are especially juicy, add up to ¼ cup more flour; take care not to add too much (the flour will look crumbly or cakey), or the filling will be pasty.

Pour the filling into the prepared crust.

MAKE THE STREUSEL: In a medium bowl, mix together the flour, brown sugar, cinnamon, salt, and vanilla with a fork. Add the melted butter and mix until incorporated and crumbly.

Use your fingers to crumble the streusel topping all over the pie. Bake until golden brown on top, 45 minutes to 1 hour; rotate the pan front to back halfway through.

INSIDER TIP • DOUBLE-CRUST PIE

For a double crust pie, make the full recipe of pie dough and divide in half. Roll each half to a round about ⅛ inch thick and 12 inches in diameter. Fit the bottom crust into the pie plate and trim the overhang to ½ inch. Fill the pie. Top the filling with the other round of dough and trim the overhang to match the bottom crust overhang. Press the overhangs together and then fold under onto the rim of the pie plate. Crimp the crust all around. Brush the crust with a little heavy cream and sprinkle with sugar. Cut an "X" right in the middle of the top crust for steam to escape. Bake as directed.

SUMMER-FRUIT CRISP

SERVES 6

Summer is the prime time for making this dessert, when the abundance of delicious fruit is just begging to be paired together in something baked. For me, the solution is often a fruit crisp—though simple, it revives the strong sense of comfort that is stored in the "just like Mom used to make" part of my brain. Crisps never disappoint, and always satisfy both the soul and the sweet tooth! I like to make them in individual gratin dishes (I use cute little mini skillets), but you could also make this in a standard baking dish.

2 cups blueberries
6 nectarines, peeled (see page 180), pitted, and sliced
5 peaches, peeled (see page 180), pitted, and sliced
1¾ cups sugar
¾ cup all-purpose flour
2 teaspoons kosher salt
1½ teaspoons ground cinnamon

1 tablespoon lemon juice
1 tablespoon vanilla extract
3 tablespoons unsalted butter, cut into small bits
Streusel from Streusel-Topped Apple Pie (page 42)
Confectioners' sugar and vanilla ice cream (optional)

Preheat the oven to 350°F.

In a large bowl, toss together the blueberries, nectarines, and peaches. Sprinkle with the sugar, followed by the flour. Using your hands or a rubber spatula, toss the fruit together to mix. Gently stir in the salt, cinnamon, lemon juice, and vanilla.

Divide the fruit mixture evenly among six small 6-inch gratin dishes or spread it all into a shallow 2½-quart baking dish. Dot the top of the fruit evenly with the butter and sprinkle with the streusel to cover.

Bake until the juices start to bubble and leak out, 15 to 25 minutes for the individuals or 20 to 30 minutes for the baking dish. Serve warm with a dusting of confectioners' sugar and a scoop of ice cream, if desired.

Candied Nuts

MAKES 2 CUPS

Nuts are candied by being simmered in a simple syrup (equal parts water and sugar) and then baked in the oven. To check if the nuts are ready to take out of the syrup, just do a touch test: Using a slotted spoon, gently fish out a nut and touch it to feel if it's tacky. If it is tacky, the nuts are ready; if not, cook a few minutes more and test again. The nuts need to simmer in the syrup long enough so that the sugar adheres to them, making them sticky.

2 cups unsalted blanched nuts (any type)	1½ cups water
	1½ cups sugar

Preheat the oven to 300°F. Line a baking sheet with a nonstick silicone liner or parchment paper.

In a 2-quart saucepan, combine the nuts, water, and sugar. Bring the mixture to a boil over high heat, then reduce the heat to a gentle simmer. Simmer until the nuts feel tacky to the touch, 10 to 15 minutes. Drain the nuts and discard the syrup.

Spread out the nuts on the lined baking sheet and bake for 10 minutes. Move the nuts around on the pan using a spoon. Return to the oven to bake until the nuts feel dry, about 15 minutes longer.

Let the nuts cool on the pan. Store airtight at room temperature.

CHOCOLATE CHERRY HAND PIES

MAKES 6

Hand pies are a fun alternative to a large pie. They travel well because they come with their own "containers," and they're great for bake sales. Hand pies have a higher crust-to-filling ratio, so it's all about having a good dough. For a fancier presentation, glaze with White Glaze (page 65) or melt some more dark chocolate and drizzle it on top.

2 cups pitted cherries (about ¾ pound
    unpitted)
½ cup sugar
1 teaspoon lemon juice
Pinch of kosher salt
2 tablespoons cornstarch

1 teaspoon vanilla extract
½ cup semisweet chocolate chips
½ recipe Simple Pie Dough (page 41),
    divided into 6 balls and chilled
Egg wash: 1 large egg beaten with
    1 teaspoon water

In a medium saucepan, combine the cherries, sugar, lemon juice, and salt. Cook over medium-low heat until the juices start to escape. Cook an additional 2 minutes, then sprinkle with the cornstarch and stir in. Cook until the liquid starts to bubble. Remove from the heat, stir in the vanilla, and let cool completely before stirring in the chocolate.

Preheat the oven to 375°F. Line a baking sheet with parchment paper.

On a well-floured surface, roll each ball of dough into a 5-inch round. Dividing the filling evenly, spoon some onto the middle of half the dough rounds, leaving about a ½-inch border of dough all around. Fold the dough in half to make half-moons. Press around the edges of the dough with a fork to seal. Brush the tops with some egg wash and place on the baking sheet.

Bake the pies until golden brown, 20 to 25 minutes; rotate the pan front to back halfway through. Transfer the pies to a wire rack to cool.

PÂTE À CHOUX

MAKES ABOUT 30 CREAM PUFFS

This pastry dough—which in French is *pâte à choux* and in English choux paste—is one of the best pastries to have in your bag of dessert tricks. It is really easy to make, but can create some incredibly impressive desserts, from éclairs and cream puffs to the showstopping St. Honoré Cake (page 173). **SPECIAL EQUIPMENT**: pastry bag, #8 plain tip

½ cup water
½ cup milk
6 tablespoons (¾ stick) unsalted
   butter
2 teaspoons vanilla extract

1 tablespoon sugar
1½ teaspoons kosher salt
½ cup + 3 tablespoons all-purpose
   flour
5 large eggs

Preheat the oven to 375°F. Line a baking sheet with parchment paper.

In a medium, deep pot, combine the water, milk, butter, vanilla, sugar, and salt. Bring to a boil. Reduce the heat to low and add the flour all at once, stirring until the mixture forms a dough. I strongly suggest using a wooden spoon for this step. Continue to stir the dough over low heat for 1½ minutes to help dry out the dough a bit. This is what starts to form the texture of the puff. When the dough starts to stick and form a slight skin on the bottom of the pot, take it off heat.

Transfer the hot dough to a stand mixer fitted with the paddle attachment and beat the dough on medium speed for about 3 minutes or until the steam stops escaping from the top of the dough. Reduce the mixer speed to low, add the eggs one at a time and beat well after each addition until fully incorporated into the dough. (The dough will break apart into pieces and look slithery, but don't worry, it comes back together.) After all the eggs have been added, beat on medium speed for 1 minute more.

At this point the dough is ready to be used in a number of different ways, but one of the commonest uses (especially in this book) is to make cream puffs.

The puffs that get used in this book are smallish, like a profiterole (if you've ever had one of those). To make the puffs, fit a pastry bag with a #8 plain tip and scoop the dough into the bag. Pipe dollops onto the baking sheet, spacing them 1 inch apart.

Bake for 15 to 20 minutes; rotate the pan front to back halfway through. Reduce the oven temperature to 325°F and bake for 10 minutes longer to help dry out the puffs.

Let the cream puffs cool on the pan before filling (see Chef It Up!, below). If making ahead, store the unfilled puffs airtight at room temperature overnight or frozen for longer storage.

chef it up!

Other than the St. Honoré Cake (page 173), which is an ultrafancy cream puff presentation, I fill cream puffs with Vanilla or Chocolate Pastry Cream (pages 77 and 78) or a Lemon Cream (page 79). To fill a puff, simply poke a hole in the bottom of the puff with the tip of a knife. Fit a pastry bag with a #2 plain tip, fill the bag with the cream, and pipe it into the puffs.

INSIDER TIP • PERFECT PUFFS

To make a beautifully shaped, restaurant-worthy cream puff, wet the tip of your finger and gently press down on the top of the unbaked puff to flatten the peak of dough that comes from piping.

SHORTCUT PUFF PASTRY

MAKES 2¾ POUNDS

Puff pastry is a staple dough, used in so many sweet and savory applications. But most people shy away from making their own because it's perceived as incredibly complicated and time consuming to make. I myself have been forced on occasion to use the store-bought frozen sheets. My pet peeve with the frozen kind is that because the dough has been folded to fit into the package, you get an unsightly seam that makes the dough puff up all wacky and uneven. Here is a homemade recipe that tastes and looks just like the real thing but is made in half the time. I've used it many times in my restaurants in a pinch, and it's a good fallback so you don't have to resort to the boxed stuff.

2 cups all-purpose flour, plus more for shaping and rolling
1 tablespoon granulated sugar
1 tablespoon kosher salt

1 pound (4 sticks) cold unsalted butter, cubed
1 cup + 3 to 4 tablespoons ice water

In a food processer fitted with the steel blade, process the flour, sugar, and salt to combine. Add the butter and process until a crumbly dough forms. (The butter will not be fully incorporated here.) Add the ice water just until the dough comes together into a shaggy mass. Turn the dough out onto a floured surface and pat out into a rectangle about 12 x 6 inches and ½ inch thick.

Fold the dough onto itself in thirds as if you were folding a piece of paper to go into an envelope, bringing one end slightly over half, then bringing in the other end.

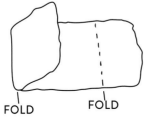
FOLD   FOLD

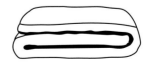

The dough will not be smooth and together at this point, but that's okay! Wrap the dough in plastic wrap and refrigerate for 30 minutes. Repeat this process of rolling out the dough to a 12 x 6-inch rectangle and making the "envelope fold" three more times. After each rolling out and folding, let the dough rest in the refrigerator for 30 minutes before you roll out and fold the dough again. Finally, roll out the dough into a 12 x 6-inch rectangle (this is now the fourth time you're doing the rolling out) and fold the two ends into the center, then fold the whole piece of dough in half, as though you were closing a book.

Wrap the puff pastry in plastic and refrigerate for at least 1 hour to firm it up before using.

chef it up!

Use this puff pastry for Palmiers (page 130) and St. Honoré Cake (page 173). The recipes do not call for the whole amount of puff pastry, but in each case you should make the entire batch of puff pastry, cut off what you need (this is a good place for a kitchen scale), and store the unused portion in the freezer.

INSIDER TIP • BUTTER

Using a high-quality butter will bring the flavor of the puff pastry to a whole new level. Choose a butter that is higher in fat than the butter commonly found in American supermarkets. Seek out European butters, if you can. My personal favorites are butters from Ireland.

LAVASH

MAKES 6 LARGE FLATBREADS

Whenever I open a new restaurant, I always enjoy serving this Italian take on the famous Turkish cracker-like flatbread known as lavash. This cheesy, salty, and slightly spicy cracker is the perfect accompaniment to drinks and makes a great nibble to have before any meal.

2⅓ cups all-purpose flour
1¼ cups whole wheat flour
3 tablespoons confectioners' sugar
1 tablespoon coarse salt, such as Maldon or kosher
2 tablespoons vegetable shortening

1¾ cups water
Extra-virgin olive oil, for greasing the pans
1 cup shredded Parmesan cheese
⅛ teaspoon cayenne pepper
Coarse sea salt, for sprinkling

In a stand mixer fitted with the paddle or dough hook attachment, mix the flours, confectioners' sugar, and salt on low speed to combine. Add the shortening and water and mix until the dough comes together and forms a ball. Mix for about 2 minutes to form the elasticity, then divide the dough into 6 equal balls.

Wrap the balls individually in plastic and let rest in the refrigerator for at least 3 hours before baking. The dough needs to relax so that it can be stretched very thin. (This dough can actually keep in the refrigerator for up to 5 days. The dough will oxidize, however, and become slightly darker in color.)

When ready to bake, preheat the oven to 370°F. Liberally grease the backs of one or two 11 x 17-inch baking sheets with olive oil. (Each piece of bread is baked on a separate baking sheet, so the more baking sheets you have, the faster this whole process will go.) Let all the dough balls come to room temperature.

(continued on page 54)

In a small bowl, toss together the Parmesan and cayenne.

Flatten a ball of dough in the middle of the baking sheet and carefully spread and stretch the dough to the edges of the pan. Let the dough hang over the sides; the goal is to stretch the dough until very thin. Don't worry if it rips or tears; this bread is meant to be uneven and "rough" around the edges. Sprinkle with a scant 3 tablespoons cheese mixture, then sprinkle with some coarse sea salt.

Bake the lavash for 10 minutes, then rotate the pan front to back, and if using 2 pans, also switch the pans from rack to rack. Bake until the dough turns a light golden brown, about 5 minutes longer. Repeat with the remaining dough.

To serve, break the bread into uneven pieces with your hands. If you've made the lavash ahead, you can freeze it in an airtight container. Recrisp it for about 8 minutes at 350°F before serving.

chef it up!

I usually fill beautiful lacquered boxes with this addictive bread and set them out on the restaurant's bar for cocktail snacking.

"EVERYTHING BAGEL" BREAD TOPPING

MAKES ABOUT 1¼ CUPS

This quick mix works well as a topping for most breads and is great to keep on hand. While you're baking the bread, brush with an egg wash (eggs beaten with a little water) about halfway through the baking time. Sprinkle the topping over the bread. I especially like to use it on the Jo Jo Bread (opposite) and Lavash (page 52) for an occasional changeup.

¼ cup poppy seeds
¼ cup sesame seeds
5 tablespoons garlic granules

3 tablespoons coarse sea salt
5 tablespoons dried onion flakes

Mix all the ingredients together. Store in a resealable plastic bag or jar in your pantry or spice cabinet.

JO JO BREAD

MAKES 32 PULL-APART ROLLS

This recipe makes me smile every time I make it because it comes from my friend Joanna, my old sous-chef. We were opening a New York restaurant and had to find a way to produce high volumes of house-made bread with very little staff and budget. We tried everything with no success, until one day she brought in this recipe from her mother and BINGO! We had a winner. The bread rises overnight in the refrigerator in a method called "cold proofing;" the cold slows down the fermentation and creates a more developed and complex flavor.

8 teaspoons active dry yeast
½ cup warm (108° to 110°F) water
4 cups bread flour
2¾ cups whole-milk cottage cheese
12 tablespoons (1½ sticks) unsalted
    butter, cubed, at room temperature
2 teaspoons kosher salt

½ cup finely chopped chives
1½ teaspoons chopped fresh rosemary
1½ teaspoons chopped fresh thyme
2 large eggs
Cooking spray
Extra-virgin olive oil, for coating
¼ cup grated Parmesan cheese

In a stand mixer fitted with the dough hook, combine the yeast and water and mix on low speed. Beat in the flour, cottage cheese, butter, salt, chives, rosemary, and thyme. On medium speed, add the eggs one at a time. Mix on high speed until the dough looks elastic. Place the dough in a large bowl coated with cooking spray. Cover and refrigerate overnight. The sticky dough "cold proofs" overnight, doubling in size and becoming firmer.

Preheat the oven to 375°F. Coat a 9 x 13-inch baking pan with cooking spray.

Punch down the dough and divide into 32 portions the size of golf balls. Arrange in the pan so they touch (this is pull-apart bread). Coat the tops with olive oil; let sit at room temperature until risen three-quarters of the way up the pan.

Sprinkle with the Parmesan. Bake until the cheese has browned and the rolls are a nice golden brown color, 30 to 40 minutes; rotate the pan front to back halfway through. Allow the rolls to cool slightly and serve warm.

PANCETTA AND GORGONZOLA SCONES

MAKES ABOUT 8 SCONES

This pancetta scone was my favorite brunch item that I developed for an Italian menu. One of my cooks, Randall, must have tested this recipe for me at least ten times before we achieved the perfect consistency and ratio of cheese to dough. Needless to say, everyone in the kitchen ate these scones for at least a week before they appeared on the menu. Our waist sizes might have grown a little, but it was well worth it. These scones are insanely tasty with this perfect combination of ingredients. Of course you can also make other scones following the same general proportions (see Variations, page 58).

1¼ cups diced pancetta (about 11 ounces)
3 cups all-purpose flour
1 tablespoon sugar
1 tablespoon baking powder
¼ pound (1 stick) cold unsalted butter, cubed

1 large egg, lightly beaten
1 cup heavy cream
1½ cups crumbled Gorgonzola cheese
Egg wash: 2 large eggs beaten with 1 tablespoon water

Preheat the oven to 325°F. Line a baking sheet with parchment paper.

In a medium skillet, cook the pancetta until crisp. Scoop out the pancetta and transfer to paper towels to drain and cool.

Much like you do with pie dough, mix all of your dry ingredients together on a work surface in a pile (see Simple Pie Dough, page 41). Next "rub" the butter into the flour mixture, using your fingertips, until the butter pieces are the size of peas. Make a well in the middle and pour in the egg and cream. Mix the ingredients together by hand until a shaggy dough is formed. Gently mix in the pancetta and Gorgonzola, kneading the dough lightly.

Pat the dough into a ½- to ¾-inch-thick rectangle. Cut the scones into 8 rect-

(continued on page 58)

angles (see Note) and arrange them on the baking sheet. Brush the tops of the scones with the egg wash. Bake until light golden brown, about 22 minutes; rotate the pan front to back halfway through.

Let the scones cool slightly on the baking sheet. Serve warm or at room temperature.

NOTE: When you cut out the rectangles, you will probably have some dough trimmings, which you can get more scones out of. However, you should gently press or stack the dough together to cut out more scones. If you compress and knead the dough back together, the end result will be tough and chewy.

VARIATIONS

Chocolate Cranberry Scones: Substitute dried cranberries for the pancetta (no need to cook them!) and 1½ cups semisweet chocolate chips for the cheese. Add the grated zest of 1 orange to the dry ingredients for the dough.

Asiago-Pepper Scones: Omit the pancetta and substitute grated Asiago cheese for the Gorgonzola. Add 2 tablespoons freshly ground black pepper to the dough.

Shortcakes: Scone dough is basically the same dough you would use for a fruit shortcake; you just need to sweeten it by adding ½ cup sugar to the dough. And of course omit the pancetta and blue cheese. Bake as directed. Top them with macerated strawberries (slice them, toss with sugar, and let sit for about 1 hour to develop juices) and Whipped Cream (page 80).

Basic Muffin Batter

MAKES 12 MUFFINS

There's nothing like a good muffin in the morning. Basic muffins are just a few simple ingredients, yet the possibilities for swap-ins and additions are endless. This recipe is just a stepping stone. Be creative and come up with your own variations. Also, check out Praline Muffins (page 60), where the basic batter gets a little boost from a sweet nut paste; Double Chocolate Chip Muffins (page 61), where cocoa powder subs in for some flour; and the truly tricked-out Carrot Streusel Muffins (page 63).

1¼ cups all-purpose flour
⅔ cup sugar
2 teaspoons baking powder
¼ teaspoon kosher salt

1 cup milk
2 large eggs
¼ cup vegetable oil

Preheat the oven to 350°F. Line the 12 cups of a muffin tin with paper liners.

In a stand mixer fitted with the paddle attachment, mix the flour, sugar, baking powder, and salt on low speed. Mix in the milk, followed by the eggs and oil, stopping to scrape the sides of the bowl with a rubber spatula to ensure that the batter is smooth and everything is combined.

Spoon the batter into the muffin cups evenly, filling them three-quarters full. Bake until they spring back to the touch and a cake tester comes out clean, 10 to 15 minutes; rotate the pan front to back halfway through. Let the muffins cool in the pan.

Vanilla Muffins: Add 1 tablespoon vanilla extract and the seeds from 1 vanilla bean to the batter.

Brown Sugar Pecan Muffins: Replace ⅓ cup of the white sugar with dark brown sugar and fold in ¼ cup pecan pieces.

Maple Walnut Muffins: Replace ⅓ cup of the white sugar with 2 tablespoons maple syrup and fold in ¼ cup walnut pieces.

PRALINE MUFFINS

MAKES 12 MUFFINS

This is a basic muffin, but with a swirl-in. Swirl-ins are a fun way to spruce up a muffin batter. For the most part, any kind of paste can be a swirl-in—from peanut butter to Nutella. Praline or hazelnut paste is available at most supermarkets with the baking ingredients. This muffin would also be great baked with a streusel topping (see page 63).

2 tablespoons light brown sugar
1½ tablespoons unsalted butter, melted

½ cup praline or hazelnut paste
1 teaspoon ground cinnamon
Basic Muffin Batter (page 59)

Preheat the oven to 350°F. Line the 12 cups of a muffin tin with paper liners.

In a small bowl, combine the brown sugar and melted butter. Mix in the praline paste and cinnamon and set aside.

Spoon the Basic Muffin Batter into the muffin cups evenly, filling them three-quarters full. Drop about 1 tablespoon of the praline mixture onto the batter and swirl it in using a tip of a knife or a skewer.

Bake the muffins until they spring back to the touch and a cake tester comes out clean, 10 to 15 minutes; rotate the pan front to back halfway through. Let the muffins cool in the pan.

DOUBLE CHOCOLATE CHIP MUFFINS

MAKES 12 MUFFINS

Notice that when the cocoa powder gets added to the basic Muffin Batter Base, the total amount of flour goes down correspondingly (see Insider Tip, below).

1 cup all-purpose flour
⅔ cup sugar
¼ cup unsweetened cocoa powder, sifted
2 teaspoons baking powder

¼ teaspoon kosher salt
1 cup milk
2 large eggs
¼ cup vegetable oil
1 cup semisweet chocolate chips

Preheat the oven to 350°F. Line the 12 cups of a muffin tin with paper liners.

In a stand mixer fitted with the paddle attachment, mix the flour, sugar, cocoa powder, baking powder, and salt on low speed. Mix in the milk, followed by the eggs and oil, stopping to scrape the sides of the bowl with a rubber spatula to ensure the batter is smooth and everything is combined. Fold in the chocolate chips.

Spoon the batter into the muffin cups evenly, filling them three-quarters full. Bake until they spring back to the touch and a cake tester comes out clean, 10 to 15 minutes; rotate the pan front to back halfway through. Let the muffins cool in the pan.

INSIDER TIP • COCOA POWDER

When you want to turn a vanilla baked good into a chocolate one, just replace some of the flour with cocoa powder. The dry, powdery cocoa behaves in a very similar fashion to flour in baked goods.

CARROT STREUSEL MUFFINS

MAKES 12 LARGE MUFFINS

Moving beyond the basic muffin, here is a fancier muffin batter with mix-ins and a streusel topping. If you're not a fan of streusel topping, you can top these instead with some Cream Cheese Frosting (page 67), which is just as delicious. **SPECIAL EQUIPMENT:** 4-ounce paper baking cups (sturdy brown paper cups available at baking supply shops)

STREUSEL
1 cup all-purpose flour
½ cup packed light brown sugar
½ teaspoon ground cinnamon
Pinch of kosher salt
6 tablespoons (¾ stick) unsalted
  butter, melted
½ teaspoon vanilla extract

MUFFINS
2 cups granulated sugar
⅓ cup + 1 tablespoon vegetable oil

3 tablespoons sour cream or crème
  fraîche
3 large eggs
1 teaspoon vanilla extract
2½ cups all-purpose flour
2 teaspoons ground cinnamon
1½ teaspoons kosher salt
1½ teaspoons baking soda
½ teaspoon baking powder
4 cups shredded carrots
¾ cup golden raisins

Preheat the oven to 350°F.

MAKE THE STREUSEL: In a medium bowl, mix together the flour, brown sugar, cinnamon, and salt. Mix in the melted butter and vanilla until crumbly. Set aside.

MAKE THE MUFFINS: In a large bowl, whisk together the granulated sugar, oil, sour cream, eggs, and vanilla until well combined. Whisk in the flour, cinnamon, salt, baking soda, and baking powder. (The batter will be thick, like a quick bread.) Using a rubber spatula, fold in the carrots and raisins.

Divide the batter among twelve 4-ounce baking cups and top each muffin with about 2 tablespoons of streusel. Bake until the muffins spring back to the touch and a cake tester comes out clean, 15 to 20 minutes; rotate the pan front to back halfway through. Let cool in the cups on a wire rack.

ROYAL ICING

MAKES ABOUT 2 CUPS

This classic icing is great for decorating both cookies and cakes. It's a must-have recipe and incredibly handy if you need to write something on your cake or cookie (see "Decorating with Icing," page 73). As the icing sits, it will dry and form a skin, so if not using it right away—or if it's on standby to be used soon—place a piece of plastic wrap directly on the surface of the icing to keep it from drying out on you and keep at room temperature.

4½ cups confectioners' sugar
3 large egg whites
1 teaspoon vanilla extract

½ teaspoon cream of tartar
Pinch of kosher salt
Food coloring of your choice

In a stand mixer fitted with the paddle attachment, mix the sugar, egg whites, and vanilla on low speed until incorporated. Stop the mixer to scrape the sides and bottom of the bowl with a rubber spatula, then add the cream of tartar and salt and continue mixing until smooth and silky.

Color the royal icing as desired. Use it right away or transfer to a container and cover the icing with a sheet of plastic wrap pressed directly on its surface. Use within 2 hours.

INSIDER TIP • FLOOD-OUT ICING

You can use royal icing to decorate large surfaces on cut-out cookies. Start by piping an outline of the shape you want with the regular royal icing. Then you "flood out" the remaining icing by adding enough water to make it runny, like a glaze. Then you pipe the flood-out icing within the lines.

WHITE GLAZE

MAKES ABOUT 3½ CUPS

G lazes are a simple and elegant way to spruce up a cake. This plain white glaze is used to decorate the Orange Buttermilk Bundt Cake (page 22) or you could drizzle it over the Chocolate Cherry Hand Pies (page 47). For a change of pace, you could swap in mint or orange extract for the vanilla.

2 cups + 2 tablespoons confectioners' sugar
5 tablespoons whole milk

2 teaspoons vanilla extract
Grated zest of 1 orange

In a bowl, whisk together the confectioners' sugar, milk, vanilla, and orange zest. If not using the glaze right away, cover the surface with plastic wrap (or a damp paper towel) so it won't form a skin. Store at room temperature.

LEMON GLAZE

MAKES ABOUT 1½ CUPS

B asically an icing that is thin enough to pour, a glaze will fall down the sides of a cake in beautiful drips. It makes an especially nice addition to a tall cake, like Angel Food Cake (page 24).

1¾ cups confectioners' sugar
Grated zest of 1 lemon

¼ cup lemon juice (1 to 2 lemons)

In a small bowl, whisk together the sugar, lemon zest, and lemon juice. If not using right away, cover the surface with plastic wrap (or a damp paper towel) so it won't form a skin. Store at room temperature.

CHOCOLATE GLAZE

MAKES ABOUT 4 CUPS

C hocolate glazes are an easy way to give a cake a professional look. To prevent the glaze from looking dull, and to give the chocolate a beautiful sheen, a little light corn syrup is added.

1 teaspoon unflavored powdered
  gelatin (a little less than ½ envelope)
5 teaspoons cold water
1½ cups semisweet chocolate chips
1½ cups heavy cream

1 tablespoon unsweetened cocoa
  powder, sifted
1 tablespoon sugar
1 tablespoon light corn syrup

In a small bowl, sprinkle the gelatin over the water to soften. Put the chocolate chips in a heatproof bowl.

In a saucepan, whisk together the cream, cocoa, and sugar. Bring to a boil. Take it off the heat and stir in the softened gelatin. Pour the hot mixture over the chocolate. Let the mixture sit for 1 minute, then stir, working from the middle outward. Finally, stir in the corn syrup.

Let the glaze cool down to just warm before working with it. You want to always glaze cakes when the glaze feels like the temperature of a warm bath.

INSIDER TIP • HOW TO GLAZE A CAKE

To glaze a cake, place the cake layer on a wire rack set over a baking sheet (to catch the drips). Gently pour the glaze around the edges of the cake and across the top, letting the excess drip down. If you missed any spots, re-glaze the spot quickly before the chocolate sets. For a restaurant-worthy glazed cake, you first give the cake layer a "crumb coat," which means to spread it with a thin, almost see-through, layer of frosting (ganache, mousse, or buttercream) to make the top and sides perfectly smooth.

CREAM CHEESE FROSTING

MAKES ENOUGH TO FROST A 9-INCH LAYER CAKE

This is my go-to icing that's always a crowd pleaser. The smooth, creamy texture with a slight tang from the cream cheese brings a great balance to any cake.

2 packages (8 ounces each) cream cheese, at room temperature
¼ pound (1 stick) unsalted butter, at room temperature

2 vanilla beans, split lengthwise
1½ cups confectioners' sugar

In a stand mixer fitted with the paddle attachment, beat the cream cheese and butter together on medium speed until smooth. Scrape in the vanilla seeds, add the sugar, and beat until smooth. Store in the fridge for up to 4 days, sealed in an airtight container. Bring the icing to room temperature before using.

INSIDER TIP • USED VANILLA BEANS
After you've used vanilla seeds in a recipe, you can save the vanilla pod, which still has a lot of flavor, and add it to a canister of sugar to make vanilla sugar. You can also use it to make your own vanilla extract (page 181), or add it to an existing batch of vanilla extract if you happen to have one going already.

FRENCH BUTTERCREAM

MAKES ENOUGH TO FROST A 9-INCH LAYER CAKE

French buttercream is by far the richest of the buttercreams with its use of egg yolks. A hot sugar syrup cooked to the soft ball stage thickens and "cooks" the egg yolks before butter is beaten in. **SPECIAL EQUIPMENT:** candy thermometer

1 cup sugar
¼ cup water
5 large egg yolks

½ pound (2 sticks) unsalted butter, cubed, at room temperature
2 teaspoons vanilla extract

In a small, deep saucepan, combine the sugar and water. Bring to a boil. Continue to cook the syrup over medium heat until the temperature reaches 238°F.

Meanwhile, in a stand mixer fitted with the whisk attachment, whip the yolks on high speed to the ribbon stage (see Insider Tip, below).

Once the syrup has reached 238°F, reduce the mixer speed to low and slowly pour the hot syrup down the side of the bowl (not onto the whisk) into the yolk mixture. Continue to whip until the mixture is no longer steaming. At this point, start adding the butter slowly. Whip on medium-high speed until it comes together. Beat in the vanilla.

INSIDER TIP • RIBBON STAGE

"Ribbon stage" describes what happens when egg yolks or a combination of yolks and sugar are whipped together. When they reach their full volume potential, they have reached the "ribbon stage." To check, lift the whisk in the air; the mixture should fall back into the bowl in a ribbon that loops back and forth on top of itself.

Buttercreams

Buttercream frosting is a staple of the pastry kitchen and a technique well worth mastering. There are several categories of buttercream, and various levels of difficulty, so start with the easier types and work your way up. But once you've made a fresh buttercream, you'll never go back to cans of store-bought frosting.

American Buttercream: The simplest of all is the American buttercream, which is just a mixture of confectioners' sugar and butter—although with commercially produced cakes (those you'll find in supermarkets and some bakeries), it's usually made with vegetable shortening. American buttercream is the type of frosting that most home cooks are probably familiar with. I do a slight variation on the idea by using cream cheese in addition to a little butter; see Cream Cheese Frosting (page 67).

French Buttercream: This frosting (opposite page) takes the idea of a simple buttercream a step further by enriching the basic frosting with egg yolks. And the sugar is added in the form of a hot syrup that cooks the egg yolks and gives the frosting body.

Then there are the meringue-based buttercreams. These produce a very white frosting and are my personal favorites. There are two types, Italian and Swiss.

Swiss Buttercream (page 70): This is the easier of the two meringue-based buttercreams and I call for it for frosting cakes in this book. It's based on what is called a Swiss meringue, which is made by heating egg whites and sugar gently in a double boiler. This not only melts the sugar but pasteurizes the whites, making them safe to eat and more shelf stable. This same method is used to make Marshmallow Creme (page 121).

Italian Buttercream (page 71): Any budding pastry chef out there might also want to master the Italian Buttercream. It is the frosting of choice for wedding cakes; it's based on an Italian meringue, which is egg whites beaten with a sugar syrup that is heated to 238°F and requires a candy thermometer.

Once you've mastered the buttercream, it's time to learn how to use a pastry bag. Just a couple of simple techniques and you'll be creating showstopping cakes. See "Decorating with Icing," page 73.

SWISS BUTTERCREAM

MAKES ENOUGH TO FROST A 9-INCH LAYER CAKE

This frosting is based on something called Swiss meringue (see "Buttercreams," page 69) and produces a lovely frosting for decorating (see "Decorating with Icing," page 73).

4 large egg whites
1 cup sugar

¾ pound (3 sticks) unsalted butter,
    cubed, at room temperature
2 teaspoons vanilla extract

In a double boiler, whisk the egg whites and sugar together until they are very hot to the touch and all the sugar has dissolved.

Pour the mixture into a stand mixer fitted with the whisk attachment and whip on medium speed until the mixture comes to medium peaks. Add the butter a cube at a time and whip until everything comes together. Beat in the vanilla. Increase the mixer speed to high and beat until the buttercream is fluffy.

VARIATIONS

Chocolate Buttercream: Melt 4 ounces semisweet chocolate chips (about ⅔ cup) in the microwave. Add all the melted chocolate at once, at the very end, after the buttercream has been whipped to fluffy.

Espresso Buttercream: Add 1 tablespoon instant espresso powder along with the egg whites and sugar in the double boiler before heating. Strain the mixture into the bowl of a stand mixer and proceed with the recipe.

ITALIAN BUTTERCREAM

MAKES ENOUGH TO FROST A 9-INCH LAYER CAKE

For an Italian buttercream, beaten egg whites are "cooked" with a hot sugar syrup before butter is added to make the frosting. The sugar syrup is heated to what is called the soft ball stage (you'll be familiar with this term if you've ever made candy). Although the actual temp for soft ball stage is 240°F, sugar syrup—much like a baked cookie— "carryover cooks." So stopping 2° earlier gives the syrup some wiggle room to continue cooking. **SPECIAL EQUIPMENT:** candy thermometer

¾ cup + 7 tablespoons + 1 teaspoon sugar
¼ cup water
½ cup egg whites (see Note)

Drop of vanilla extract (or more to taste)
10 ounces + 2 tablespoons unsalted butter, cubed, at room temperature

In a small, deep saucepan, combine ¾ cup plus 2 tablespoons of the sugar and the water and bring to a boil. Continue to cook the syrup over medium heat until the temperature reaches 238°F.

Meanwhile, in a stand mixer fitted with the whisk attachment, beat the egg whites on low speed while gradually adding the remaining 5 tablespoons plus 1 teaspoon sugar. Beat in the vanilla.

Once the sugar syrup has reached 238°F, slowly pour the syrup along the side of the egg white bowl while the mixer is going at low speed. Make sure you don't get the syrup on the moving whisk, as it is very hot and you can get burned. Continue to whip the whites to full volume or stiff peaks.

While still whipping, slowly add the butter, whipping until all the butter has been added. The whites will deflate and fall, but when you continue to whip it will come back together and fluff back up.

NOTE: Crack egg whites into a liquid measuring cup until you get to ½ cup. You'll need about 3 eggs.

Decorating with Icing

Decorating with icing is by far the most fun and exciting part of the cake-making process. However, it can be extremely challenging if you're not sure how to use decorating tools properly. Here are some tips on using decorating tips and some easy go-to cake decorating how-to's for an impressive iced cake.

TIPS ON TIPS

The key piece of equipment for cake decorating is the tip—the small metal cone that fits in the bottom of a pastry bag. The tip is placed in the bag before it's filled with whatever you will be piping. The two basic and most-used tips are known as the plain (or straight) tip and the star tip. A plain tip has just a round hole that comes in various diameters, and it can create beads of icing or smooth lines. The star tip is a multiple-pronged tip used for piping a ridged line, rosettes (see opposite page), and the ever-popular shell border. These are really the only two tips you need for basic decorating. There are, of course, some super specialized tips, like a "grass tip" with many little holes that create the texture and look of grass. And the #2 pastry tip used to fill pastries like cream puffs, éclairs, or doughnuts. It's a long, thin, straight tube that pokes a hole in the pastry and then pipes in the filling without letting any leak out.

GO-TO DECORATING MOVES

If you learn just these two tricks, you'll be golden.

Rosettes: Piping a rosette is very simple but always looks classy and stunning. Using a #30 star tip, pipe the icing through the tip in a tight circular motion, almost piping its tail on top of itself (see the photo at left). To cover an entire cake in rosettes, pipe them in vertical lines across the top and down the sides. This creates a ruffled fabric look.

Petals: To make frosting "petals," you will need a #6 or #7 plain (straight) tip and a small off-set spatula. Starting on the side of the cake, pipe a vertical line of "pearls" (beads of icing). Using the small offset spatula, gently pull a pearl outward like a smear, creating a small petal. Continue to do this for all the pearls on the line. Pipe the next set of vertical pearls where the tails of the first petals end. Repeat this process all the way around the sides of the cake, including the top. To see the finished product, see the photo on page 15.

MAKE YOUR OWN CORNET

When you need to pipe a very thin line, like if you are adding intricate detail or filigree, or if you're writing something like "Happy Birthday" on a cake, you need a cornet, which is small piping bag that gives you really fine control over the icing. It's easily assembled from parchment paper (but you could also use plain old computer paper). Best of all? There's no washing up. Here's how you make a cornet.

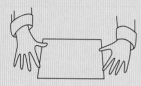

1. Cut a rectangular piece of parchment paper. The size doesn't matter here, just needs to be a rectangle.

2. Next fold the paper along the longest diagonal, from corner to corner. You will end up with something that is straight along one side and looks like two side-by-side mountain peaks on the opposite side.

3. Cut the paper along the fold, creating two elongated triangles. You only need one of the triangles to make a cornet, but you might need a second cornet, so don't throw away the other half of the paper.

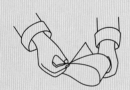

4. Hold the triangle so that the longest of the three sides is facing to the left and the original corner of the paper (the 90 degree angle) is facing to the right. Curl the short end point (at the top) down and around to meet the 90 degree angle corner. You will see that this has formed a cone.

5. Wrap the longer, bottom point around the cone and bring it up to meet the other points. Wiggle and pull at the points of the cone until you have made an absolutely tight and sharp tip. Tuck in the points to hold the cone in place.

6. Fill with your icing and roll the bag up tightly (like rolling up a tube of toothpaste) on the side opposite the seam, to pull the seam taut and keep it closed. Cut a tiny hole in the tip and pipe.

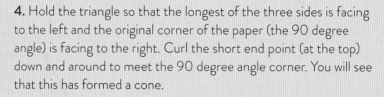

GANACHE FILLING

MAKES ENOUGH TO FILL AND FROST A 9-INCH LAYER CAKE

G anache is the term for a filling or glaze made by heating cream and chocolate together and emulsifying it by stirring. This is my basic recipe; however, don't be fooled into thinking it's easy—ganache can be a bit temperamental. You can make a ganache well ahead, refrigerate it, and melt it down when you need it.

2⅓ cups semisweet chocolate chips   2½ cups heavy cream

Place the chocolate chips in a heatproof bowl. In a small saucepan, bring the cream to a boil. Pour the hot cream over the chocolate. Let the mixture stand for 30 seconds, then stir the mixture until it comes together. Let the mixture stand at room temperature until it sets to a spreadable consistency, about 1 hour. Slightly whisk it to thicken.

Store in the refrigerator if not using right away, but you'll have to remelt it (see Insider Tip, below) when you're ready to use it.

VARIATION
Mocha Ganache: Add 2 tablespoons instant espresso powder to the cream in the saucepan before you bring it to a boil.

INSIDER TIP • HOW TO REMELT A GANACHE
You will not be able to spread a cold ganache, so it needs to be gently, partially remelted. To do this, put the ganache in a metal bowl and place it directly over a low flame. When a little of the ganache melts at the bottom of the bowl, whisk it up into the rest of the ganache to loosen it up. Repeat the process (if necessary) until the ganache reaches spreading consistency.

PEANUT BUTTER FILLING

MAKES ENOUGH TO FILL A 9-INCH LAYER CAKE

This can be used as a filling for a cake, but it also works well as a topping on various desserts like cupcakes and puddings. The best part is that it's so easy to make. It's reminiscent of a peanut butter cup filling—in fact, it makes a great filling for a molded chocolate. Or try it on my Brownie Fluff-a-Nutter (page 21).

1 cup confectioners' sugar
¼ pound (1 stick) unsalted butter, at
   room temperature

2 cups creamy peanut butter

In a stand mixer fitted with the paddle attachment, beat together the sugar and butter on medium speed until smooth. Add the peanut butter and mix on medium speed until smooth.

Store the filling at room temperature if using the same day, or in the fridge in an airtight container for up to 5 days. Bring back to room temperature before using if it was refrigerated.

chef it up!

The peanut butter filling also makes a great truffle. Once the filling is refrigerated and firmed up, you can scoop it with a small cookie scoop and roll the mixture into balls. Refrigerate the balls again before coating them in chocolate. For my slightly messy, but really effective, method of coating truffles with melted chocolate, see page 111. Top the chocolate-coated balls with a small pinch of coarse sea salt before the chocolate sets.

VANILLA PASTRY CREAM

MAKES ABOUT 6 CUPS

Pastry cream is a must-have recipe for everyone's collection. It's a base filling for pastries like éclairs and cream puffs. With its neutral taste, you can flavor it with anything from chocolate to liquor. In this book, I use it in my Banana Cream Pie (page 39), in the cream puffs in St. Honoré Cake (page 173), and between the layers in the Black and White Crêpe Cake (page 183).

¾ cup sugar
4 large egg yolks
¼ cup cornstarch
4 cups whole milk

Pinch of kosher salt
2 teaspoons vanilla extract
5 tablespoons unsalted butter, cubed

In a small bowl, whisk together 6 tablespoons of the sugar, the egg yolks, and cornstarch.

In a medium saucepan, combine the milk, salt, and the remaining 6 tablespoons sugar. Bring to a boil. Using a ladle, pour in small amounts of the hot liquid while whisking to temper the egg yolks (see "Tempering Eggs," page 78).

Add the tempered egg yolk mixture back to the hot milk and continue to whisk over medium-low heat until the pastry cream starts to bubble, about 5 minutes. Once it starts to bubble, cook for 1 minute more, whisking constantly. Take it off the heat and stir in the vanilla and butter.

Transfer the pastry cream to a bowl and set the bowl in an ice bath (a larger bowl filled with ice and water). Place a piece of plastic wrap touching the surface of the cream so that it doesn't form a skin as it cools. After the cream is fully cooled, you can keep it in the refrigerator for up to 1 week.

INSIDER TIP • STABILIZE YOUR BOWL!
Place a wet paper towel underneath a bowl to keep it from wobbling as you whisk.

CHOCOLATE PASTRY CREAM

MAKES ABOUT 6 CUPS

Use this to fill cream puffs (page 48). Once the pastry cream is made, place a piece of plastic wrap touching the surface of the cream so that it doesn't form a skin as it cools. After the cream is fully cooled, you can keep it in the refrigerator for up to 1 week.

¾ cup sugar
4 large egg yolks
¼ cup cornstarch
4 cups whole milk
Pinch of kosher salt

2 teaspoons vanilla extract
2 tablespoons semisweet chocolate chips
5 tablespoons unsalted butter, cubed

In a small bowl, whisk together 6 tablespoons of the sugar, the egg yolks, and cornstarch.

In a medium saucepan, combine the milk, salt, and the remaining 6 tablespoons sugar. Bring to a boil. Using a ladle, pour in small amounts of the hot liquid while whisking to temper the egg mixture (see Insider Tip, below).

Add the warmed egg yolk mixture back to the hot milk and continue to whisk over medium-low heat until the pastry cream starts to bubble, about 5 minutes. Once it starts to bubble, cook for 1 minute more, whisking constantly. Take it off the heat and stir in the vanilla, chocolate chips, and butter.

Transfer the pastry cream to a bowl and set the bowl in an ice bath (a larger bowl filled with ice and water).

INSIDER TIP • TEMPERING EGGS

To combine a hot liquid and eggs or egg yolks, you need to warm ("temper") the eggs first. A boiling liquid added to cold eggs would scramble them and make them unusable. So first whisk a little hot milk into the eggs, then whisk the warmed, tempered eggs back into the hot liquid.

LEMON CREAM

MAKES ABOUT 8 CUPS

This basic lemon cream recipe can be used for many dessert applications. You can use it as a cake filling or a topping. Or use just the lemon curd (without the whipped cream folded in) in a tart or lemon meringue pie.

1 tablespoon unflavored powdered
   gelatin (a little more than
   1 envelope)
¼ cup cold water
1¾ cups sugar
1 tablespoon grated lemon zest
5 large eggs

4 large egg yolks
1½ cups lemon juice (about 8 lemons)
1 cup sour cream
½ pound (2 sticks) unsalted butter,
   cubed
2 cups heavy cream, whipped to stiff
   peaks

In a small bowl, sprinkle the gelatin over the water to soften.

In a medium saucepan, combine the sugar, lemon zest, whole eggs, egg yolks, lemon juice, and sour cream and heat gently, whisking constantly, until the mixture thickens enough to coat the back of a spoon. Do not let it boil. It will bubble once or twice, but do not overcook or you risk actually scrambling the eggs. Stir in the softened gelatin until melted.

With a hand blender (or in a stand blender), blend in the butter and continue to blend until the mixture cools down a bit. Transfer to a bowl and place a piece of plastic wrap directly on the surface to keep a skin from forming. Refrigerate for at least 4 hours or overnight.

When ready to use, fold in the whipped cream.

INSIDER TIP • BLOOMING GELATIN

The term for softening gelatin before you use it is "blooming," which, although it describes the swelling of the gelatin when it's combined with cold water, actually comes from a man named Bloom, who developed a test for the gelling strength of gelatin.

WHIPPED CREAM

MAKES ABOUT 6 CUPS

For the best results when making whipped cream, the cream, bowl, and beaters should all be nice and cold. Chill the mixer bowl and whisk in the refrigerator or freezer for about 10 minutes prior to whipping.

2 cups well-chilled heavy cream
½ cup confectioners' sugar

2 teaspoons vanilla extract

In a stand mixer fitted with the whisk attachment, start whipping the cream on low speed. When the cream just begins to gain volume, slowly add the sugar and vanilla. Continue to whip on medium speed until stiff peaks form.

VARIATIONS

Cinnamon Whipped Cream: Add 1 tablespoon ground cinnamon when you add the vanilla.

Brandied Whipped Cream: To make about 3 cups, use 1 cup cream, ¼ cup confectioners' sugar, and 1 teaspoon vanilla. Add 1 tablespoon brandy when you add the vanilla.

INSIDER TIP • RESCUING OVERWHIPPED CREAM

If you whip cream for too long, eventually you'll end up with butter. If you start to find yourself in this predicament, there's an easy fix: Just lightly whip in some new unwhipped heavy cream and you will see your whipped cream magically restored.

CALVADOS CARAMEL SAUCE

MAKE 4 CUPS

This is my basic caramel sauce recipe that I always use at my restaurants. The addition of Calvados (French apple brandy) is optional—you could use apple cider in its place—but I like the depth of flavor it adds. Caramel sauce keeps well, so this is definitely a make-ahead recipe that you could always have on hand. You can use it on ice cream or drizzle it over cake slices.

2 cups sugar
½ cup light corn syrup
1½ cups heavy cream

Pinch of kosher salt
2 tablespoons unsalted butter
½ cup Calvados

Place the sugar in a deep saucepan. Pour in the corn syrup (it should be enough to cover the sugar by ¼ inch). Cook over medium heat until medium-dark brown, about 10 minutes. Stirring constantly with a wooden spoon, gradually add the cream. Be very careful as the mixture will bubble up in the pan as you add the cream. This is extremely hot! Stir in the salt and butter and take it off the heat.

Strain the caramel through a fine-mesh sieve into a large heatproof container. Using a hand blender, blend in the Calvados and refrigerate.

VARIATION

Spiced Caramel Sauce: Add 2 teaspoons ground cardamom or cinnamon and omit the Calvados.

CHOCOLATE SAUCE

MAKES 2 CUPS

This recipe is for a basic, all-purpose chocolate sauce. Its thick and smooth dark chocolate consistency is reminiscent of the Smucker's hot fudge ice cream topping I had as a child. It makes a great gift—put it in a beautiful jar with some ribbon—for any chocolate lover.

¼ cup sugar
½ cup + 2 tablespoons water
½ cup light corn syrup
¼ cup unsweetened cocoa powder, sifted

½ cup bittersweet chocolate chips
4 tablespoons (½ stick) unsalted butter, cubed
1½ teaspoons vanilla extract
¼ teaspoon kosher salt

In a large saucepan, combine the sugar, water, corn syrup, and cocoa. Bring to a boil over medium-high heat. Add the chocolate chips and butter. Whisk constantly until the butter and chocolate have melted. Reduce the heat to medium and cook for about 12 minutes to thicken it up a bit. Stir in the vanilla and salt.

Let the sauce cool before storing in the refrigerator.

VARIATIONS

Chocolate-Mint Sauce: Add 1 tablespoon crème de menthe or 2 teaspoons mint extract (in addition to the vanilla). If you use extract, taste and see if you need more since brands of extracts can vary widely in strength.

Chocolate-Orange Sauce: Add 1 tablespoon Grand Marnier or 2 to 3 teaspoons orange extract (in addition to the vanilla). If you use extract, taste and see if you need more since brands of extracts can vary widely in strength.

Chocolate-Whiskey Sauce: Add 1 tablespoon whiskey (your choice).

Raspberry-Chocolate Sauce: Stir in ½ cup freeze-dried raspberries.

RASPBERRY COULIS

MAKES ABOUT 2 CUPS

E very summer, my grandmother would take me to a local farm where we would buy fresh raspberries. She would buy 2 pints, one for snacking on immediately and the other to make the sauce for our favorite peach Melba dessert. After going to culinary school, I learned that my grandmother's simple, delicious sauce had a much fancier name: coulis. Here is a basic coulis recipe that can be used to make any kind of fresh berry sauce. Always taste the berries you're using for sweetness; you may have to adjust the sugar. And if you choose to make this with blackberries, you absolutely must not skip the seed-straining step. The seeds are enormous.

½ cup sugar
1 tablespoon lemon juice

1 pint raspberries

In a blender, puree all the ingredients on low speed. Strain the sauce to remove the seeds. Store in the refrigerator.

VARIATION
Peach Melba Not exactly a variation on the raspberry sauce so much as a bow to my grandmother's annual summer dessert. Make the Raspberry Coulis (I mean the Melba sauce). Spoon it over a scoop of Vanilla Ice Cream (page 108) along with some macerated fresh peaches. To macerate the peaches, peel them (see "Peeling Peaches," page 180), slice them, and toss them with a little sugar. Let them sit for at least 1 hour at room temperature to develop juices.

BEYOND
Baking

A pastry chef's responsibilities span more than just baking. We are required to know how to make everything from custard to candies. In this chapter, you will find recipes for crêpes, sorbets, fancy candies, puddings, and even fried desserts such as zeppole. (You might be surprised at how popular fried desserts are . . . or maybe not!)

Classic Hot Cocoa Mix (page 117)

CRÊPES

MAKES ABOUT 20 CRÊPES

Crispy-edged and as delicate as a flower petal, crêpes are a great way to get creative and wow your guests. The batter is so easy to make—and the best part is you can fill a crêpe with almost anything, sweet or savory. See Chef It Up! (page 88) for a couple of suggestions. Or try making the classic Crêpes Suzette (page 89). And of course, no crêpe talk would be complete without a recipe for Black and White Crêpe Cake (page 183), a great showstopping dessert.

1½ cups + 2 tablespoons whole milk
2 tablespoons unsalted butter, melted
¾ cup all-purpose flour
1½ teaspoons sugar
½ teaspoon kosher salt

2 large eggs
2 tablespoons seltzer water
¾ teaspoon vegetable or grapeseed oil
¼ teaspoon vanilla extract

In a saucepan or in the microwave, heat the milk until warm.

Transfer the warmed milk to a blender, add the melted butter, and blend on low speed. Blend in the flour, sugar, and salt. Add the eggs one at a time, blending well after each addition. Blend in the seltzer, oil, and vanilla. Refrigerate the mixture for 4 to 5 hours before using, preferably overnight (see "Give the Batter a Rest," page 88).

Preheat an 8-inch nonstick skillet over medium-high heat. **NOTE:** *It's important to have your pan good and hot in order to get a thin, delicate crêpe.* Using a 2-ounce (¼-cup) ladle or scoop, pour the batter (it should only be a small amount) onto the hot pan and swirl the pan around so the batter makes a thin pancake. It should almost be see-through. The crêpe will start to cook and crisp on the edges first; give it about 1½ minutes, then use a small offset spatula to flip the crêpe over to brown slightly on the other side. The color will be pale brown on both sides when it's cooked through and ready.

(continued on page 88)

As you work, stack the crêpes, putting pieces of paper towel or parchment paper between them so they don't stick to one another. If you don't need all of the crêpes or don't need them right away, you can refrigerate or freeze them.

chef it up!

Nutella Crêpes: Spread about 1 tablespoon Nutella in the center of a crêpe. Top the crêpe with sliced strawberries or bananas. Fold in two sides to create a sort of cone shape (see photo, page 86). Garnish with more fruit.

Honey-Ricotta Crêpes: Spread blackberry jam over the crêpes. Top with ricotta sweetened with a little honey. Fold the crêpes in half and then in half again (to form quarter-circle wedges). Sprinkle with confectioners' sugar.

INSIDER TIP • GIVE THE BATTER A REST

The reason that crêpe batter has to "rest" before you use it is that as the batter sits in the refrigerator, the flour absorbs some of the moisture and swells, creating a more luscious, cohesive, and emulsified batter.

CRÊPES SUZETTE

SERVES 4

Whenever I think of Crêpes Suzette I start to laugh. You see, in college I did a summer internship at a casino, and the casino often held huge events in the grand ballrooms. Being at the bottom of the totem pole and the least experienced, I often got to do all the grunt work. On the Fourth of July, my boss handed me a Betsy Ross costume and told me that I was working an action crêpe station dressed as Betsy . . . and he added, "Try to remain in character." I looked so ridiculous: The costume was about three sizes too big, and I doubted anyone's image of Betsy Ross included cooking crêpes. As humiliating as it was, I can say I made over 200 crêpes that day, totally perfecting my technique. So it wasn't a total loss!

8 Crêpes (page 87), cooked; see Note below

5 tablespoons unsalted butter, cubed

6 tablespoons packed light brown sugar

2 tablespoons orange juice

2 tablespoons Grand Marnier

Fold each crêpe in half, then fold in half again (to form quarter-circle wedges).

In a 10-inch skillet, combine the butter and brown sugar over medium heat and heat until melted. Stir in the orange juice and let simmer for about 15 seconds. Working in batches, place the folded crêpes in the pan and toss them in the sauce.

Take the pan off the heat and add the Grand Marnier. Place the pan back on the heat to warm through. Serve the crêpes warm.

NOTE: The crêpe recipe makes more than you need for this dessert. The options are to cut the batter in half and make fewer crêpes; or make the entire batch and freeze what you don't use or refrigerate the extra crêpes to have for breakfast the following day

ZEPPOLE

MAKES ABOUT 20 ZEPPOLE

I always tell people that I'm a "splish splash." I'm Italian, Irish, Polish, and German. It's the Italian part that loves this dessert. Nothing says delicious comfort food more to me than zeppole. I make my zeppole with ricotta, which is not the traditional way. The ricotta makes the batter a little looser, and it gives a wonderfully moist result at the end. In restaurants, I would often send these to a table for an anniversary or birthday with an espresso as a fun way to end a celebratory meal. **SPECIAL EQUIPMENT**: deep-frying thermometer or a deep fryer; spider

About 6 cups vegetable oil, for
   deep-frying
¾ cup all-purpose flour
1 tablespoon sugar
1½ teaspoons baking powder

¼ teaspoon kosher salt
2 large eggs
1 cup whole-milk ricotta cheese
2 teaspoons vanilla extract
Confectioners' sugar, for dusting

Fill a medium, deep pot with enough vegetable oil to come up 3 inches (or use a deep fryer if you have one). Heat the oil to 350°F.

While the oil is heating, in a bowl, whisk together the flour, sugar, baking powder, and salt. Whisk in the eggs, ricotta, and vanilla until a smooth batter forms.

Working in batches, drop tablespoons of batter (about 5 zeppole at a time) into the hot oil. They will sink to the bottom, then rise to the top before browning. When they are a deep golden brown, after about 6 minutes, use a spider or slotted spoon to transfer them to paper towels to drain briefly.

While they are still warm, toss them in confectioners' sugar. Serve warm.

chef it up!

I always like to serve these to my guests in brown paper bags, the way they do at fairs. And I don't sugar the zeppole first. I put a shaker of powdered sugar on the table so the guests can sugar their own. It's very nostalgic.

COCONUT CUSTARD

MAKES ABOUT 4 CUPS

Coconut custard just sings summertime dessert to me. This custard recipe is so simple to make, but the applications for it can be endless. Sometimes I'll use this custard as a cake filling or I'll set it with a bit of gelatin (see Chef It Up!) and serve it as a molded dessert.

1 cup half-and-half
1 can (14 ounces) coconut milk
5 large egg yolks
¾ cup sugar
2 tablespoons cornstarch

2 tablespoons unsalted butter
1 tablespoon coconut-flavored rum
2 teaspoons vanilla extract
Pinch of kosher salt

In a medium saucepan, combine the half-and-half and coconut milk and bring to a boil.

While the mixture is heating, in a small bowl, whisk together the egg yolks, sugar, and cornstarch.

Temper the egg yolk mixture by gradually whisking in the hot cream mixture. Pour the entire mixture back into the pan and cook over medium heat until thick and creamy, about 5 minutes.

Take the custard off the heat and stir in the butter, rum, vanilla, and salt. Transfer to a bowl set into an ice bath (a larger bowl of ice and water) and set aside to chill.

chef it up!

To make little molded desserts with the custard, soften 1 envelope (¼ ounce) unflavored powdered gelatin in ¼ cup cold water. Stir the softened gelatin into the hot custard to dissolve. Spoon the custard into eight 4-ounce ramekins and refrigerate for at least 4 hours to set. Sprinkle the tops of the custard with granulated sugar (about ⅛ inch thick). Torch the top with a crème brûlée torch until a medium-gold color. Serve topped with Blueberry Compote (opposite page).

BLUEBERRY COMPOTE

MAKES ABOUT 2½ CUPS

Compotes have been used widely around the world for hundreds of years as inexpensive desserts. Traditionally served over clotted cream with crumpets, nowadays compotes are seen on seasonal pastry menus everywhere as a component of modern desserts. On my menus I've used this same compote recipe for every fruit from strawberry to blackberry and even rhubarb. There is nothing I love more than a great swap-out recipe like this one.

2 cups fresh or thawed frozen blueberries
½ cup sugar
Grated zest and juice of 1 orange

1 tablespoon light corn syrup
1 tablespoon water
Small pinch of kosher salt

In a medium saucepan, combine the blueberries, sugar, orange zest and juice, corn syrup, water, and salt. Bring to a simmer over medium heat and cook until the blueberries start to burst and pop, about 5 minutes. Reduce the heat to low and cook for 2 minutes more.

Let the mixture cool to at least room temperature before serving.

chef it up!
Compotes don't always have to be used as a topping. Try using a compote as a swirl-in for the Plain Cheesecake (page 30). Use 1 to 1½ cups of the compote, depending on how blueberry-ish you want the batter. Serve the cheesecake topped with Whipped Cream (page 80).

The Magic of Custard

E ggs, milk, and sugar combine to make a host of desserts, from rich ice creams (see Vanilla Ice Cream, page 108) to custards like crème caramel or Coconut Custard (page 92). Custard is also used to make French toast and as a binder for desserts like bread pudding (which is really just deconstructed baked French toast).

CAKE PUDDING

SERVES 8 TO 10

The idea of "cake pudding" came to me when I had been experimenting with pound cakes and had tons of it just sitting there. I could not bring myself to throw any away. Then, the "aha" moment. I swapped in the cake for bread in my bread pudding recipe—and voilà! Cake pudding was a hit at the restaurant staff meal and a regular for me at home. I also discovered that leftover muffins are as good as pound cake in this easy dessert. By the way, this would be a good place to use leftover Orange Buttermilk Bundt Cake (page 22) . . . if there is any.

8 (1-inch) slices pound cake or
   6 standard-size muffins (any flavor
   will do), cut into 1-inch cubes
4 large eggs
4 large egg yolks
¾ cup sugar
2 cups heavy cream

2 cups whole milk
1 vanilla bean, split lengthwise
Pinch of kosher salt
2 cups butterscotch chips or
   semisweet chocolate chips (optional)
Ice cream, for serving

Preheat the oven to 350°F. Arrange the cake in a 9 x 13-inch baking pan in one layer.

In a medium bowl, whisk together the whole eggs, egg yolks, and sugar; set aside.

In a medium saucepan, combine the cream and milk. Scrape in the vanilla seeds and add the vanilla bean halves and salt. Whisking all the while, slowly pour the hot cream mixture into the egg mixture to temper it. Pour the custard back into the pan. Continue to whisk the custard over medium heat for 1 minute longer. Discard the vanilla bean halves. Pour the custard over the cake cubes. Mix in the chips, if using. Bake until the custard has set, about 40 minutes.

Cut into rectangles or squares. Serve warm with a scoop of ice cream.

PAIN PERDU

SERVES 8 TO 10

We call it French toast. The French call it *pain perdu*. But whatever you call it, the bread and custard combo is always a hit. Although most people think of this as breakfast, I make it for dessert, with a rich custard (heavy cream and some extra egg yolks) and thick-cut bread—either an enriched bread like challah or brioche, or baguette. There are two keys to success when making pain perdu: First, let the bread soak in the custard just long enough to saturate the middle; it shouldn't be soggy. Second, always cook it in a hot pan; too cold a pan will not yield the beautiful, even golden crust. And use salted butter to cook the bread—the salt balances the flavors (bread can be bland) and helps with the browning.

2 cups heavy cream
4 large eggs
2 large egg yolks
2 tablespoons honey (I prefer clover)
1 tablespoon vanilla extract
2 tablespoons all-purpose flour

½ teaspoon ground cinnamon
Pinch of kosher salt
9 thick (1- to 1½-inch) slices bread
Salted butter, for cooking
Confectioners' sugar and fresh fruit,
    for serving

In a blender, combine the cream, whole eggs, egg yolks, honey, vanilla, flour, cinnamon, and salt on low speed. Pour the mixture into a square pan or a shallow dish (large enough to fit more than one bread slice, if possible). Working in batches, soak the bread for about 1 minute on each side and set aside in a clean pan.

In a 10-inch nonstick skillet, melt enough butter to coat the bottom of the pan over high heat. Place as many slices of bread as will fit without overlapping and cook for about 1 minute or until golden brown. Flip the slices over and cook for about 1 minute on the other side. If the pan gets too hot, turn the heat down to medium-low until the temperature goes down a little. Repeat with the remaining bread and more butter.

Serve warm topped with a dusting of confectioners' sugar and fresh fruit.

Pain Perdu with Orange-Glazed Bananas: Make the Pain Perdu and while it's cooking, melt 6 tablespoons (¾ stick) unsalted butter with ⅓ cup packed light brown sugar in a saucepan. When the sugar just starts to bubble, add ⅓ cup orange juice. Gently fold in 2 bananas, sliced ¼ inch thick. Cook for about 1 minute to reduce the sauce. To serve, spoon some glazed bananas over each slice of French toast and sprinkle each serving with some butterscotch chips or milk chocolate chips.

CHOCOLATE PANNA COTTA

SERVES 8

I n Italian, *panna cotta* simply means cooked cream. There is something to be said about how Italian desserts are just so simple and yet so soul satisfying. I've been known to make panna cotta in all kinds of flavors, from this chocolate version to brown sugar (page 99) to Meyer lemon. Panna cotta is an easy and quick make-ahead dessert. Just set it and forget it!

1 envelope (¼ ounce) unflavored powdered gelatin (2½ teaspoons)
¼ cup cold water
2¾ cups heavy cream
¾ cup sugar
½ cup unsweetened cocoa powder, sifted
1 tablespoon semisweet chocolate chips
½ teaspoon vanilla extract
Pinch of kosher salt

In a small bowl, sprinkle the gelatin over the water to soften.

In a medium saucepan, whisk together the cream, sugar, and cocoa. Bring to a boil over medium heat.

Take the cream mixture off the heat and whisk in the chocolate chips, vanilla, softened gelatin, and salt. Whisk until everything has melted. Pour the mixture into eight 4-ounce molds or ramekins and refrigerate for at least 3 hours to set.

To unmold, gently pull the panna cotta away from the sides of the ramekin with your finger as you invert the panna cotta onto a plate. Serve chilled.

chef it up!

S'More Panna Cottas: Make the panna cotta in ramekins and top each serving with about 1 tablespoon store-bought or homemade Marshmallow Creme (page 121); torch with a crème brûlée torch. Sprinkle the top of the creme with crushed graham crackers.

Hibiscus Gelée

The term gelée, in the restaurant world, is used to describe a liquid set with gelatin. Sound familiar? That's right: It's a more refined term for Jell-O. Gelées are trendy in the dessert world today and used not as the star of the dessert, but as a garnish. You can finely chop it (called an *hachée*) and use it to garnish a dessert plate to give it some pop, or use it to top a panna cotta (see opposite page and page 96) . The chopped gelée catches the light and looks like little crystals. This is the perfect opportunity for swap-outs: See some suggestions below.

> 5½ teaspoons unflavored powdered gelatin (2 envelopes + ½ teaspoon)
> 2½ cups water
>
> 2 cups sugar
> 3 hibiscus teabags

In a small bowl, sprinkle the gelatin over ½ cup of the water to soften.

In a saucepan, combine the remaining 2 cups water and the sugar. Bring to a boil. Cook until the sugar dissolves. (This is the simple syrup.)

Add the hibiscus teabags to the simple syrup and bring it back to a boil. Take it off the heat. Add the gelatin to the hot syrup and stir to dissolve the gelatin. Cool to room temperature. Discard the teabags and pour the liquid into a 1-quart container. Refrigerate for 4 hours to set.

Invert onto a cutting board and roughly cut into little crystal shapes.

Coffee Gelée: Use 2½ cups brewed coffee in place of the water and hibiscus tea.

Apple Gelée: Use 2½ cups unsweetened apple juice or apple cider in place of the water and hibiscus tea. Reduce the sugar to ½ cup.

Mango Gelée: Use 2½ cups mango nectar in place of the water and hibiscus tea. Reduce the sugar to ½ cup.

BROWN SUGAR PANNA COTTA

SERVES 8

Here is another favorite variation on panna cotta. You can also make a simple vanilla bean panna, which goes well with anything, just by swapping out the brown sugar and using white sugar.

1 envelope (¼ ounce) unflavored
   powdered gelatin (2½ teaspoons)
¼ cup cold water
3⅔ cups heavy cream

½ cup packed dark brown sugar
1 vanilla bean, split lengthwise
Pinch of kosher salt

In a small bowl, sprinkle the gelatin over the water to soften.

In a medium saucepan, combine the cream and brown sugar. Scrape in the vanilla seeds and add the vanilla bean halves. Bring to a boil over medium-high heat.

Take the cream mixture off the heat, discard the vanilla beans halves, and whisk in the softened gelatin and salt. Whisk until everything has melted. Pour the mixture into eight 4-ounce molds or ramekins and refrigerate for at least 3 hours to set.

To unmold, gently pull the panna cotta away from the sides of the ramekin with your finger as you invert the panna cotta onto a plate. Serve chilled.

chef it up!
Unmold the panna cotta onto a plate and top with candied pecans (see "Candied Nuts," page 46). Serve with a small scoop of pear sorbet.

RED WINE–POACHED PEARS
WITH MASCARPONE CREAM

SERVES 6

Poached fruits always look beautiful and make for a great presentation. This easy dessert is perfect for a light end to a heavy meal. You can serve the pears as is if you don't want to make the mascarpone cream.

PEARS
4 cups red wine
4 cups water
2 cups granulated sugar
2 cinnamon sticks
1 vanilla bean, split lengthwise
3 Bosc pears, peeled, halved
   lengthwise, and cored

MASCARPONE CREAM
1 cup mascarpone cheese
½ cup heavy cream, chilled
2 teaspoons vanilla extract
1 cup + 1 tablespoon confectioners'
   sugar

POACH THE PEARS: In a medium saucepan, combine the wine, water, sugar, and cinnamon sticks. Scrape in the vanilla bean seeds and add the vanilla bean halves. Bring to a boil over high heat. Add the pears and reduce the heat to a simmer. Simmer until the pears just begin to soften, about 10 minutes.

Take out the pears and set them aside. Discard the cinnamon sticks; rinse and dry the vanilla bean halves and save for another use (see page 67). Transfer the poaching liquid to a bowl set in an ice bath (a larger bowl filled with ice and water). When the poaching liquid has cooled fully, return the pears to it. Refrigerate and serve chilled. (The fruit will keep, covered, for up to 8 days in the refrigerator.)

MAKE THE MASCARPONE CREAM: In a stand mixer fitted with the whisk attachment, whip the mascarpone with the cream and vanilla extract. Slowly add the confectioners' sugar while whipping to stiff peaks.

Serve a chilled pear half with a dollop of mascarpone cream in the hollowed-out core. Drizzle with some of the poaching liquid.

Poaching Fruit

Poaching is a form of cooking that lets you infuse lots of flavor into fruit by simmering it in liquid. Now to the fun part: You can use almost any type of liquid! What follows are some basic poaching liquids; note the ratios of wine/juice to water to sugar—when you scale the poaching liquid up or down, keep these ingredients in the same proportions. The wine- and juice-based poaching liquids are used for hard fruits, such as pears (see Red Wine–Poached Pears, page 101), apples, or quince. This amount of poaching liquid will be enough for 4 pieces of fruit that have been halved (a total of 8 halves). You can also poach soft fruits, but it takes a different method. See "Poaching Soft Fruit," opposite page.

WINE POACHING LIQUID

For a red wine poaching liquid, add whole spices like cinnamon sticks, whole cloves, and cardamom pods. White wine poaching liquid is great with vanilla bean, but also spices such as whole cloves and cardamom pods.

4 cups red or white wine   2 cups sugar
4 cups water

In a medium saucepan, combine the wine, water, and sugar. Bring to a boil over high heat. Add the fruit of choice, then reduce the heat to a simmer. Take the fruit out of the hot liquid just when it begins to soften (this will vary with the type of fruit and its ripeness).

Discard any spices that were used. Transfer the poaching liquid to a bowl set in an ice bath (a larger bowl filled with ice and water). When the poaching liquid has cooled completely, return the fruit to it. Refrigerate and serve chilled. (The fruit will keep, covered, for up to 8 days in the refrigerator.)

To make a syrupy sauce out of the poaching liquid, transfer it to a small saucepan and simmer until it's reduced by half. Let the sauce to cool to room temperature before serving.

FRUIT JUICE POACHING LIQUID

Great with spices, depending on the fruit juice. Cinnamon sticks and nutmeg are great with apple juice, and I would use cardamom pods with pomegranate.

5 cups fruit juice, such as orange, apple, or pomegranate

3 cups water
2 cups sugar

In a medium saucepan, combine the fruit juice, water, and sugar. Bring to a boil over high heat. Add the fruit of choice, then reduce the heat to a simmer. Take the fruit out of the hot liquid just when it begins to soften (this will vary with the type of fruit and its ripeness).

Discard any spices that were used. Transfer the poaching liquid to a bowl set in an ice bath (a larger bowl filled with ice and water). When the poaching liquid has cooled completely, return the fruit to it. Refrigerate and serve chilled. (The fruit will keep, covered, for up to 8 days in the refrigerator.)

To make a syrupy sauce out of the poaching liquid, transfer it to a small saucepan and simmer until it's reduced by half. Let the sauce to cool to room temperature before serving.

POACHING SOFT FRUIT

Soft fruits such as citrus, berries, peaches, and melon are poached in a simple syrup (equal parts water and sugar, boiled to dissolve the sugar). In this method the fruit is not cooked in the poaching liquid to soften it, because it's already soft. Instead, the warm (not hot) syrup is poured over the fruit. The fruit then sits in the syrup for at least 1 hour, but can keep in the refrigerator for up to 8 days. You can get creative with the simple syrup, too, by adding tea or spices, or even stirring in some liquor. I like to use a little Campari to flavor the syrup I pour over grapefruit segments.

BLACKBERRY SORBET

MAKES ABOUT 1 QUART

Sorbet consists of three basic ingredients: water, sugar, and fruit juice. What makes a sorbet either good or bad depends on its texture. And the texture depends on the sugar level, which you test with something called "buoyancy" (see "The Buoyancy of an Egg," page 106). This recipe is one example of a sorbet base. Feel free to use other fruits, but always check the sugar levels; this technique is the most important thing. Place the container you're going to store the sorbet in in the freezer before you begin to process the base. This will keep the sorbet from melting when you scoop it out of the ice cream machine.

3 cups water
3 cups sugar

1 pound blackberries
1 raw egg (uncracked and washed well)

In a small saucepan, bring the water and sugar to a boil, stirring to dissolve the sugar. Set the simple syrup aside to cool.

In a blender or food processor, process the blackberries to a smooth puree. Push the puree through a fine-mesh sieve into a bowl. Discard the seeds.

Whisk 1 cup of the simple syrup into the blackberry juice. Carefully drop in the egg. If the egg does not float, add more simple syrup, ½ cup at a time. Once the egg floats just enough to show a quarter-size circle of shell, the sorbet base is ready.

Transfer the base to an ice cream machine or a stand mixer ice cream attachment and freeze according to the manufacturer's directions. Transfer the sorbet to a covered container and place in the freezer.

VARIATION

Passion Fruit Sorbet: Use 2 cups unsweetened passion fruit puree in place of the blackberry juice.

RASPBERRY SHERBET

MAKES ABOUT 1½ QUARTS

Many people ask me what's the difference between sorbet and sherbet and the answer is: the addition of dairy. Sherbet is simply a sorbet with milk or cream added. Here is a sherbet recipe using most of the same ingredients as in the sorbet base on page 104.

4 cups water
4 cups sugar
1 pound raspberries

1 cup whole milk
1 raw egg (uncracked and washed well)

In a small saucepan, bring the water and sugar to a boil, stirring to dissolve the sugar. Set the simple syrup aside to cool.

In a blender or food processor, process the berries to a smooth puree. Push the puree through a fine-mesh sieve into a bowl. Discard the seeds. Whisk the milk into the raspberry juice.

Whisk 1 cup of the simple syrup into the raspberry juice. Carefully drop in the egg. If the egg does not float, add more simple syrup, ½ cup at a time. Once the egg floats just enough to show a quarter-size circle of shell, the sherbet base is ready.

Transfer the base to an ice cream machine or a stand mixer ice cream attachment and freeze according to the manufacturer's directions. Transfer the sherbet to a covered container and place in the freezer.

INSIDER TIP • THE BUOYANCY OF AN EGG

Too little sugar and a sorbet will be too icy, and too much is also a turn-off. Finding just the right amount comes down to the buoyancy of an egg. When the right amount of sugar is added, an egg will float to the surface of the mixture, revealing a bit of the eggshell the size of a quarter. Because not every fruit has the same degree of natural sugar, it's imperative to check the sugar level of the sorbet base before you start churning.

HUCKLEBERRY FROZEN YOGURT

MAKES ABOUT 5 CUPS

Frozen yogurt is much like a sherbet in the fact that it's a sorbet base with the addition of a dairy product, in this case Greek yogurt. This is another great swap-out recipe. The huckleberry juice can be swapped out for another type of fruit juice. With frozen yogurt being so trendy lately, this one is sure to be a hit.

1 pound huckleberries or blueberries, stemmed
2½ cups water

2 cups sugar
2 cups + 2 tablespoons Greek yogurt

In a medium saucepan, combine the huckleberries and ½ cup of the water. Cook over medium-high heat until the berries burst, 6 to 8 minutes. With a hand blender (or in a stand blender), puree the berries. If there are seeds, push the puree through a fine-mesh sieve into a bowl. Discard the seeds.

In a medium saucepan, combine the sugar and the remaining 2 cups water. Bring to a boil, stirring to dissolve the sugar. Transfer the simple syrup to a blender.

Add the yogurt and huckleberry juice to the hot simple syrup and blend until completely smooth. Refrigerate until completely cool.

Transfer the chilled base to an ice cream machine or a stand mixer ice cream attachment and freeze according to the manufacturer's directions. Transfer to a freezer container and freeze.

VANILLA ICE CREAM

MAKES 1½ QUARTS

Who doesn't love ice cream? I surely appreciate it because I've essentially made a living out of the stuff. The technique for making ice cream is not difficult; however, making a great ice cream instead of just a good ice cream is all about the ingredients. For example, organic milk and cream have more of a viscous body to them, which helps achieve the smooth, creamy texture that every ice cream maker so desperately tries to achieve. And if you can find unhomogenized organic milk, even better. If you're making a vanilla ice cream, vanilla beans will give a tastier result than extract. And for chocolate ice cream (see the variation on the opposite page), seek out a high-end chocolate with more cocoa butter (also known as couverture chocolate).

1½ cups organic heavy cream	6 large egg yolks
1½ cups organic whole milk	¾ cup sugar
1 vanilla bean, split lengthwise	1 tablespoon light corn syrup

In a medium saucepan, combine the cream and milk. Scrape the vanilla seeds into the pan and then add the vanilla bean halves.

In a bowl, whisk together the egg yolks, sugar, and corn syrup. Add a small ladleful of the cold cream-milk mixture to the egg yolks and whisk to combine.

Bring the remaining cream-milk mixture to a boil over medium heat.

Whisking constantly, ladle small amounts of the hot cream-milk mixture into the yolk mixture until it feels warm, then pour it all back into the saucepan. Cook the custard over low heat, stirring constantly in a figure-8 pattern, until it thickens slightly and coats the back of a spoon (see Insider Tip, opposite page).

Set up an ice bath (a large bowl of ice and water). Strain the custard mixture into a bowl that will fit in the ice bath. Stir occasionally as it chills, then transfer to the refrigerator until well chilled. Discard the vanilla bean.

Transfer the ice cream base to an ice cream machine or a stand mixer ice cream attachment and freeze according to the manufacturer's directions. Transfer the ice cream to a freezer container and place in the freezer until you're ready to serve. Let sit at room temperature briefly before serving.

VARIATIONS

Chocolate Ice Cream: Omit the vanilla seeds and bean and whisk 2 tablespoons unsweetened cocoa powder into the milk-cream mixture. After the custard has been cooked and coats the back of a spoon, stir 4 ounces of finely chopped couverture chocolate into the hot mixture until melted. Strain and freeze as directed. Personally, I go for dark chocolate, but you can substitute milk chocolate and take out 1 tablespoon of the sugar to balance the sweetness.

Espresso Ice Cream: Add 2 tablespoons espresso powder to the milk and cream mixture in the saucepan.

INSIDER TIP • NAPPÉ

In the professional kitchen, the French term *nappé* is used to describe the stage at which a mixture that is being thickened over heat will coat the back of a spoon. A good way to check if you've come to the nappé point is to dip the spoon in the mixture to coat and then run your finger down the middle of the back of a spoon. If the line holds its shape, you have reached nappé.

CHOCOLATE TRUFFLES

MAKES 40 TO 50 TRUFFLES

C hocolate truffles are one of the most versatile confections you can make. With these easy recipes, you can get as creative as you want using different flavorings (see Chef It Up!, page 112, for some of my favorites). Notice the ratio of chocolate to cream in each recipe creates the perfect texture for that specific truffle.

DARK CHOCOLATE TRUFFLES
1 cup semisweet chocolate chips, plus
    1 pound (about 2⅔ cups) for coating
½ cup heavy cream
¼ teaspoon kosher salt
Unsweetened cocoa powder, for
    dusting

MILK CHOCOLATE TRUFFLES
1 cup milk chocolate chips, plus
    1 pound (about 2⅔ cups) for coating
⅓ cup + 1 tablespoon heavy cream

¼ teaspoon kosher salt
Ground blanched hazelnuts (see "Nut
    Flours" page 29), for dusting

WHITE CHOCOLATE TRUFFLES
1 cup white chocolate chips, plus
    1 pound (about 2⅔ cups) for coating
¼ cup heavy cream
¼ teaspoon kosher salt
Unsweetened shredded coconut, for
    dusting

Place the 1 cup chocolate chips in a heatproof bowl.

In a small saucepan, bring the cream and salt to a boil. Pour the hot cream over the chips and let sit for 30 seconds. Stir until the chips are completely melted and blended with the cream. This is the ganache. Refrigerate for at least 4 hours and up to overnight so that the ganache firms up enough to be scooped and formed into truffles.

In a double boiler or in the microwave (see Insider Tip, next page), melt the 1 pound chocolate chips for coating. Line a baking sheet with parchment paper.

This gets messy, but if you want to make truffles the way I do, here it is: Spread the dusting mixture (cocoa, coconut, or nuts) out on a second rimmed

(continued on page 112)

baking sheet. Scoop the ganache mixture out using a melon baller and roll into balls. Dip both your hands in the melted chocolate, coating your palms. Roll the truffle between your chocolaty hands to make a thin layer of coating. Then drop the coated truffle into the dusting mixture and shake the pan to roll it around. Leave all the truffles in the dusting mixture until you're done coating, then wash your hands. Transfer the truffles to the parchment-lined baking sheet to set. Let set at room temperature, then store in an airtight container in the refrigerator.

chef it up!

Milk Chocolate Chai Truffles: When the cream comes to a boil, add 2 chai teabags. Let steep for 1 hour until the flavor is strong enough. Discard the teabags. Bring the cream back to a boil for melting the milk chocolate chips.

Strawberry Daiquiri Truffles: Grind 1½ cups freeze-dried strawberries to a powder in a mini food processor or blender. Make the melted chocolate mixture for the White Chocolate Truffles. After you've melted the chocolate, stir in the strawberry powder, 2 tablespoons white rum, and 2 teaspoons lime juice.

INSIDER TIP • CHOCOLATE IN THE MICROWAVE

Melting chocolate in the microwave takes a little fussing because the chocolate doesn't lose its shape as it softens, so you don't have a visual cue that it's melted. So what you have to do is melt it on high power in short blasts (like about 10 seconds) and try to stir the chocolate after each blast to see if it's soft.

Chocolate Can Be Cranky

Chocolate is one of life's most decadent pleasures. One can't even imagine what the world of pastry would be without it—or my mood swings for that matter. Chocolate can also be one of the most complicated ingredients to work with. Just like people, different chocolates have different personalities, which determines how you should treat them.

Dark chocolate: I refer to dark chocolate as the Employee of the Month of chocolates. It is by far the easiest to work with and manipulate. It has less cocoa butter in it than other chocolates, which means when you're melting it you can heat it for longer without risk of burning or overheating.

Milk chocolate: This is the middle child of chocolate (no offense to middle children). It's caught between dark chocolate and white. It's the best of both worlds and also the worst of both worlds. It tends to melt a little bit faster than dark chocolate, so keep this in mind while melting. Check it earlier then you think you should.

White chocolate: This is the most temperamental of the three and needs to be handled gently. I like to say "treat white chocolate like a lady." When melting white chocolate, it's good practice to stir the chocolate often, even removing it from the heat while stirring. It's the very high cocoa butter content that makes white chocolate burn so easily and quickly.

Seizing: This is the ultimate chocolate crankiness. A chocolate that has "seized" turns lumpy, thick, and impossible to melt. Seizing can be caused by two things: 1) Overheating or 2) moisture—if even a drop of liquid hits the melted chocolate, it'll seize right up. Unfortunately there is no way to recover seized chocolate (though it's still edible; you just can't cook with it). My advice? Stop and start over.

CREAMSICLE FUDGE

MAKES 16 PIECES

Nowadays everyone makes fudge the easy, shortcut way using store-bought marshmallow creme (see page 121 for my homemade version). I'm all in favor of shortcuts when they make sense, but I find that type of fudge too sweet and sometimes grainy. The old-fashioned fudge that I grew up with on the boardwalks of the Jersey Shore is a simple combination of cooked sugar syrup and chocolate that gets beaten slightly as it cools to incorporate a small amount of air and build a smooth texture. This fudge is smooth and creamy and melts in your mouth. **SPECIAL EQUIPMENT:** candy thermometer

Cooking spray
3 cups sugar
2 tablespoons light corn syrup
1 tablespoon glucose (available in baking supply stores; see Insider Tip, page 116)
1¼ cups heavy cream

4 tablespoons (½ stick) unsalted butter
2 or 3 drops orange extract
1 teaspoon vanilla extract
¾ cup white chocolate chips
1 or 2 drops orange food coloring

Line the bottom and sides of a 4 x 8-inch loaf pan or a 5 x 7-inch or 6 x 6-inch baking pan with foil, leaving an overhang so you can pull the fudge out. Lightly coat the foil with cooking spray.

In a medium saucepan, stir together the sugar, corn syrup, glucose, cream, and butter and cook, without stirring, over medium heat. Let the syrup cook until it reaches 238° to 240°F, what's known as the "soft ball stage." If the sugar syrup starts to crystallize along the sides of the pot, you can use a wet pastry brush to dissolve the sugar and wipe down the sides. The object here is to not incorporate the sugar crystals that form; if you do, you will end up with grainy fudge. Once the syrup has reached its temperature, stir in the orange and vanilla extracts and pour the syrup into the bowl of a stand mixer fitted with

(continued on page 116)

the paddle attachment. Beat on medium-low speed until slightly cooled and thickened, 6 to 10 minutes. While the machine is running and the syrup is still warm, beat in the white chocolate chips.

Measure out one-third of the mixture and transfer to a separate bowl. Beat the orange food coloring into the fudge remaining in the mixer bowl. Pour the orange fudge into the prepared pan, then dollop the white mixture onto the orange. Drag the tip of a knife or a toothpick through it to marbleize.

Let the fudge cool and set in the pan for at least 6 hours. Pull out of the pan and cut into squares or rectangles. The fudge can be stored in an airtight container for 5 to 7 days.

INSIDER TIP • GLUCOSE

As a professional pastry chef, I know that one of the biggest problems with cooked sugar mixtures is "crystallization." This is what happens when a sugar solution has more sugar than the syrup can handle and some of the sugar sort of un-dissolves and reverts to its crystalline state. A sugar syrup that crystallizes will cause whatever is made with it to be grainy. To avoid the problem, I add some glucose to my sugar syrup; the glucose prevents the crystals from forming. Look for glucose in baking supply stores, shops that sell candy-making supplies, or online.

The Art of Gift-Giving

In the restaurant business, it's a necessity to impress your guests and leave them with a great feeling so that they'll come back again. I like to send people home with little gifts like small cakes, chocolates, or my favorite in the winter, hot cocoa mix. There's no reason you shouldn't do this for your friends, too.

CHOCOLATE-CARAMEL HOT COCOA MIX

MAKES 20 (¼-CUP) SERVINGS

Here's a homemade cocoa mix that won't be easily forgotten by your giftee. It's made with homemade caramel powder! Be sure that you include these instructions with your gift: "For 1 mug of hot cocoa, stir ¼ cup of mix into ¾ cup boiling water (top with marshmallows)."

1 cup sugar
2 cups nonfat dry milk powder
¾ cup unsweetened cocoa powder, sifted

½ cup powdered nondairy creamer
Pinch of kosher salt
1 cup butterscotch chips
Miniature marshmallows (optional)

Line a baking sheet with parchment paper or a nonstick silicone liner.

In a small saucepan, heat ¼ cup of the sugar over medium-high heat, stirring until it caramelizes to a medium brown color, about 10 minutes. Pour the caramel out onto the lined pan and let cool completely. Break up the caramel and grind to a fine powder in a food processor.

In a large bowl, whisk together the caramel powder, milk powder, cocoa, nondairy creamer, salt, butterscotch chips, and the remaining ¾ cup sugar.

Divide the mix among cute containers, such as small vintage canning jars. Top with miniature marshmallows, if desired. The mix will keep at room temperature up to 2 months.

Classic Hot Cocoa Mix: For a simpler version, skip the caramel powder. Use only ¾ cup sugar and replace the butterscotch chips with semisweet chocolate chips. All the other ingredients remain the same, as do the brewing instructions.

The Next LEVEL

The recipes in this chapter are not necessarily more difficult to put together (many of them use the same basic techniques that you'll find in "Baking 101"), but they all represent a greater commitment of time (like PB&J Whoopie Pies, page 120) and/or equipment (like Brown Butter Pizzelle, page 135). In some cases, they're about building on basic techniques and inventing something new. One of the best feelings in baking is when you dream up an idea for a dessert and you have enough knowledge to make it happen. This chapter is all about taking the basics to another level.

PB&J Whoopie Pies (page 120)

PB&J WHOOPIE PIES

MAKES 12 PIES

L ike cupcakes and cake pops, whoopie pies have become a trendy dessert recently. I had never had one until I tried to make them myself, and instantly thought of this variation. They were as fun to make as they are a fun play on two common foods. Of course as a chef, I like to give the whoopie pies a little extra visual appeal. I fill a pastry bag (fitted with a #4 star tip) and pipe the filling in a giant rosette (see page 73) on the bottom cookie. Then I top with the second cookie and gently squish until the ridged filling just shows at the sides.

COOKIES
2¼ cups cake flour
1 teaspoon baking powder
1 teaspoon baking soda
½ teaspoon kosher salt
½ cup vegetable shortening
½ cup creamy peanut butter
½ cup packed light brown sugar
2 large eggs
1½ teaspoons vanilla extract

1½ cups half-and-half

FILLING
1 cup vegetable shortening
1 cup confectioners' sugar
Pinch of kosher salt
1 teaspoon vanilla extract
1½ cups marshmallow creme, store-bought or homemade (page 121)
½ cup grape jam or jelly

Position one oven rack in the top third of the oven and a second rack in the bottom third. Preheat the oven to 375°F. Line 2 baking sheets with parchment paper.

MAKE THE COOKIES: In a bowl, whisk together the flour, baking powder, baking soda, and salt.

In a stand mixer fitted with the whisk attachment, cream the shortening, peanut butter, and brown sugar. Beat in the eggs one at a time, then beat in the vanilla. Alternate adding the half-and-half and the flour mixture in several additions.

Using a 2-ounce (¼-cup) cookie scoop, place the batter on the baking sheets 2 inches apart. These cookies will, and are meant to, spread. Bake until light golden brown, 9 to 11 minutes; halfway through, switch the pans from rack to rack and also rotate the pans front to back. Transfer to a wire rack to cool.

MAKE THE FILLING: In a stand mixer fitted with the paddle attachment, beat the shortening with the confectioners' sugar, salt, and vanilla on medium-high speed until smooth. Reduce the speed to medium-low and beat in the marshmallow creme and jam. Scrape the sides with a rubber spatula as you work.

After the cookies have cooled, spread a generous amount of the filling on the flat side of one cookie, then top with another cookie, flat side down. These will keep, covered, in an airtight container for up to 1 week.

chef it up! MAKE YOUR OWN MARSHMALLOW CREME
MAKES ABOUT 3 CUPS

As a little girl, I had two strange, sugary obsessions that I'm not really proud of: powdered iced tea mix and marshmallow creme, both of which I just ate right off a spoon. I eventually grew out of my addictions, but my love for "fluff" has continued well into my career. I find ways to make it my own and use it on desserts all the time. This recipe is so simple to make—and you can top virtually anything with marshmallow creme to make the ordinary extraordinary. For some added flair, if you have a crème brûlée torch, toast the marshmallow creme for a nod to childhood memories of sitting around the campfire!

½ cup egg whites (see Note)	Dash of vanilla extract
1 cup sugar	

In a double boiler over simmering water, whisk the eggs whites with the sugar until the sugar is completely dissolved and the mixture is very hot to the touch.

Transfer the mixture to a stand mixer fitted with the whisk attachment. Beat until stiff peaks form. Beat in the vanilla at the very end. Store the creme at room temperature.

NOTE: In this recipe, the ratio of sugar to egg whites (2:1) is extremely important. So separate your egg whites into a liquid measuring cup and stop when you get to ½ cup. You'll need somewhere between 2 and 3 large eggs.

CIDER DOUGHNUTS

MAKES 36 DOUGHNUTS

When I wake up in the morning, I usually have little time to think about breakfast. Anyone who works in a restaurant can tell you that you get very little sleep from the time you get home to the time you have to be back at work. Breakfast is often just a cup of coffee. However, I do make these doughnuts on special occasions for breakfast, and for dessert as well. **SPECIAL EQUIPMENT:** deep-frying thermometer or a deep fryer; doughnut cutter or two round cutters, one about 2¼ inches in diameter and the other about 1¼ inches; spider for turning

1½ cups packed light brown sugar
1 teaspoon ground cinnamon, plus
   2 tablespoons for dusting
1 teaspoon grated nutmeg
½ teaspoon ground allspice
½ teaspoon kosher salt
½ pound + 4 tablespoons unsalted
   butter, at room temperature

5 large eggs
2½ cups apple cider
11 cups all-purpose flour
5 teaspoons baking powder
1 teaspoon baking soda
Vegetable oil, for deep-frying
1 cup granulated sugar

In a stand mixer fitted with the paddle attachment, beat together the brown sugar, 1 teaspoon of the cinnamon, the nutmeg, allspice, and salt on medium speed. Add the butter a bit at a time and beat until well incorporated. Reduce the speed to low and add the eggs one at a time, beating well after each addition. Beat in the cider.

In a large bowl, whisk together the flour, baking powder, and baking soda. Slowly add the flour mixture to the batter, beating until the mixture comes together; you will end up with a moist dough.

Line an 11 x 17-inch rimmed baking sheet with parchment paper. Scrape the dough onto the sheet. Top with another sheet of parchment paper and use

(continued on page 124)

a rolling pin to spread out the dough to ½ inch thick. Refrigerate for 2 hours to firm up the dough for cutting.

In a heavy-bottomed, deep saucepan, pour in enough vegetable oil to come up 3 inches (or use a deep fryer, if you have one). Heat the oil to 350° to 375°F.

While the oil is heating, cut out doughnuts using a doughnut cutter or two round cutters (one smaller than the other). Save the little center pieces to fry up as extra treats. Pat the scraps back together to ½ inch thick and cut out more doughnuts.

In a medium bowl, whisk together the 2 tablespoons cinnamon for dusting and the granulated sugar, and have at the ready. Line a baking sheet with paper towels.

Working in batches of 4 or 5 (whatever fits comfortably in the pot without crowding), add the doughnuts to the hot oil. They will sink and then rise to the top. Turn them carefully with a spider and cook until a deep golden brown, about 2 more minutes. Remove the doughnuts from the oil with the spider and drain on the paper towels. Be sure to let the oil come back to at least 350°F before cooking the next batch.

Toss the warm doughnuts in the cinnamon-sugar and serve warm.

chef it up!

I love to serve these doughnuts with my Calvados Caramel Sauce (page 81) for dipping. Serve the sauce in a coffee cup for a cute riff on coffee and doughnuts.

INSIDER TIP • ALWAYS TEST

I always make the first doughnut (or any fried dough) my test subject. I can judge by its color, but I make sure to cut it open to see if it's cooked through. This helps me better gauge the timing for the rest. After each batch, be sure to wait about 1 minute for the oil to come back up to temp before adding any more doughnuts.

FIG & WALNUT CAKE

MAKES ONE 9-INCH CAKE

I n my role as restaurant pastry chef I always look to showcase seasonal ingredients, so when fresh figs start showing up (in the Northeast) in the summer, and all the way into the fall, I make this rich and spicy cake. I'm not a big fan of the seedy texture figs can have, so for this cake I puree them, which gives the cake moistness with just the perfect hint of natural sweetness. The cake needs no frosting and pairs perfectly with just a simple sweetened whipped cream. This is truly my favorite way to eat figs!

Cooking spray
1 cup sugar
¼ cup grapeseed oil
2 large eggs
½ teaspoon vanilla extract
½ teaspoon ground cinnamon
½ teaspoon ground cloves
½ teaspoon grated nutmeg

½ teaspoon baking soda
¼ teaspoon salt
¼ cup half-and-half
1 cup cake flour, sifted
1 cup pureed fresh figs (about 1 pint figs)
½ cup chopped pecans
½ cup confectioners' sugar, for dusting
½ recipe Whipped Cream (page 80)

Preheat the oven to 350°F. Line the bottom of a 9-inch cake pan with a parchment paper round and coat the pan and paper with cooking spray.

In a stand mixer fitted with the paddle attachment, beat the sugar and oil together on medium speed. Reduce the speed to low, add the eggs one at a time, beating well after each addition. Beat in the vanilla. Beat in the cinnamon, cloves, and nutmeg, then beat in the baking soda and salt. Alternate beating in the half-and-half and cake flour in several additions, ending with flour. Finally, beat in the fig puree and pecans.

Bake for 12 minutes. Rotate the pan front to back and bake until a cake tester comes out clean, about 12 minutes. Let cool in the pan.

To serve, invert the cake onto a cake plate. Dust the top with confectioners' sugar. Serve warm or at room temperature with a dollop of the whipped cream.

MAPLE PUMPKIN CHEESECAKE

SERVES 12 TO 16

This is a stunning cheesecake, perfect for the fall holidays. To get a leg up on your holiday baking, you can make this well ahead and freeze it (cheesecakes freeze really well). But don't be a crazy person and try to make your own pumpkin puree—canned puree is always perfect and consistent. Serve the cheesecake with a dollop of Cinnamon Whipped Cream (page 80; make only ½ recipe). If you can get it, use Grade B or D maple syrup (see Insider Tip, opposite page) for a much deeper flavor.

Graham Cracker Crust (page 30)
with 1 tablespoon ground cinnamon
added
4 packages (8 ounces each) cream
cheese, at room temperature
1½ cups sugar
5 large eggs
¾ cup sour cream, at room
temperature

¼ cup heavy cream, at room
temperature
3 tablespoons dark maple syrup
2 cups canned pumpkin puree (not
pumpkin pie filling)
2 teaspoons pumpkin pie spice
2 teaspoons vanilla extract
¼ cup all-purpose flour
1 tablespoon grated lemon zest

Prepare and bake the crust as directed. Set aside to cool. Leave the oven on.

In a stand mixer fitted with the paddle attachment, beat the cream cheese on medium speed until creamy, about 2 minutes. Beat in the sugar, eggs, sour cream, heavy cream, maple syrup, pumpkin puree, pumpkin pie spice, vanilla, flour, and lemon zest until blended. Stop and scrape the bowl often.

Choose a roasting pan that will hold the springform pan. Place the roasting pan on a pulled-out rack in the oven. Place the springform pan in the center of the roasting pan and carefully pour in the batter. Pour hot water into the roasting pan (staying well away from the springform, so you don't get any water into the cheesecake batter) to come halfway up the sides of the springform pan. Gently slide the rack back into place and close the oven door.

Bake until the center slightly jiggles, about 1 hour 20 minutes. Turn off the oven and leave the cheesecake inside to completely cool, about 6 hours. Take it out of the water bath, cover, and refrigerate for at least 4 hours or overnight. Remove the pan sides and cut into slices.

INSIDER TIP • THE SYRUP COUNTS

Did you know that maple syrups are graded? The typical supermarket syrup is usually Grade A, but you can also find Grade B (and sometimes Grade D). These are much stronger in their maple flavor, and really worth seeking out (and spending some extra money for). But if you can't find those—they're definitely available in maple syrup country, and in high-end gourmet shops—be sure that you buy "pure" maple syrup. The syrups that are simply labeled "pancake syrup" are maple imposters. They're really just sugar syrups dressed up with maple flavor and some caramel coloring. That said, if the cute little lady-shaped bottle is all you have on hand, by all means use it, but just add in a bit more to get more maple flavor.

NO-BAKE RICOTTA CHEESECAKE

SERVES 10 TO 12

I always thought of ricotta cheesecake as an overbaked, crumbly abomination, compared to standard cheesecake. All the memories I had of eating it were just "ehhh" and not really enjoyable. In my family, we always had it at the end of our Easter ham dinner—also not my favorite meal, but I digress. It was fate; I knew what I had to do: I had to reinvent the technique for making ricotta cheesecake. After about twelve different versions, I decided that a no-bake cheesecake was the way to go. The addition of white chocolate and cream cheese in this recipe helps to add to the creamy texture and has almost removed the now faint and distant memory of what I once knew as ricotta cheesecake. The reinvention was a success and proved to be a hit on my restaurant menu!

COOKIE CRUST
Cooking spray
¼ cup amaretti cookie crumbs (you can find these cookies in most supermarkets)
¾ cup all-purpose flour
¼ cup packed light brown sugar
Pinch of kosher salt
¼ pound (1 stick) unsalted butter, melted

FILLING
¾ cup whole-milk ricotta cheese
6 ounces cream cheese
½ cup granulated sugar
1 tablespoon grated orange zest
1¼ teaspoons kosher salt
1 teaspoon vanilla extract
1 vanilla bean, split lengthwise
½ cup white chocolate chips, melted
1 envelope (¼ ounce) unflavored powdered gelatin (2½ teaspoons)
¼ cup cold water
2 cups heavy cream, chilled

MAKE THE CRUST: Preheat the oven to 325°F. Line the bottom of a 10-inch springform pan with a parchment paper round and coat the paper with cooking spray.

In a medium bowl, mix together the cookie crumbs, flour, brown sugar, salt, and melted butter. Firmly pack and press the crust into the springform pan going ½ to 1 inch up the sides. Bake for 12 minutes to set the crust. Let the curst cool completely.

MAKE THE FILLING: In a stand mixer fitted with the paddle attachment, beat the ricotta and cream cheese on medium speed until smooth and fluffy. Add the granulated sugar, orange zest, salt, and vanilla extract. Scrape the seeds out of the vanilla bean into the bowl. (Save the vanilla bean halves for another use; see page 67.) Continue to beat the mixture until light and fluffy. Once the mixture is smooth, add the melted white chocolate all at once and blend.

In a small microwave-safe bowl, sprinkle the gelatin over the water. Let stand for 5 minutes to soften. Place the bowl in the microwave and cook on high for about 30 seconds to dissolve. Add the dissolved gelatin to the ricotta mixture and continue to beat for 30 seconds. Scrape the filling into a large bowl. Wash and dry the mixer bowl.

In a stand mixer fitted with the whisk attachment, whip the heavy cream to stiff peaks. Using a rubber spatula, gently fold the whipped cream into the filling until evenly combined. Pour the filling into the baked crust and refrigerate at least 3 hours.

Remove the pan sides and cut into slices.

chef it up!

I like to serve this cheesecake with orange segments that have been poached in simple syrup (see "Poaching Soft Fruit," page 103) along with a scoop of orange sorbet.

PALMIERS

MAKES 18 COOKIES

Palmiers (which means "palm trees" in French) are a wonderful marriage of sophisticated and simple. Also known as elephant ears, palmiers are sugary, buttery treats that not only look gorgeous but just melt in your mouth, the perfect accompaniment to a cup of coffee.

¾ cup sugar
2 teaspoons ground cinnamon
1 teaspoon kosher salt

8 ounces puff pastry, store-bought or homemade (page 50; see Note)

In a small bowl, mix the sugar, cinnamon, and salt.

Sprinkle a work surface with 2 tablespoons of the sugar mixture. Using a rolling pin, roll the pastry into a 10 x 15-inch rectangle, a little less than ⅛ inch thick. (If using store-bought pastry, which is already rolled out, just roll it a bit to get the sugar to adhere and to make it a little thinner.) Sprinkle a thin layer of the sugar mixture on top of the dough to evenly cover. Starting at one short end, fold in the pastry in thirds until it reaches the middle. Repeat with the other side. Then fold the two halves in, as though you were closing a book. Wrap the dough in plastic wrap and refrigerate for 30 minutes to firm it up for slicing.

Preheat the oven to 375°F. Line a baking sheet with parchment paper or a nonstick silicone liner.

Cut the rolled cookie log crosswise into ¼-inch-thick slices. Lay them on the baking sheet about 2 inches apart.

Bake for 10 minutes, then flip the cookies over and bake until they turn a medium caramel color, about 10 minutes longer. Transfer the cookies to a wire rack to cool.

NOTE: Make the full recipe of puff pastry, measure out what you need for this recipe (about one-fourth of the total), and freeze the remaining pastry for another use.

CHOCOLATE BISCOTTI

MAKES ABOUT 40 COOKIES

Being known as an Italian pastry chef, I've had to make my fair share of biscotti. The thing that I love the most about this recipe is that it's so versatile. I've added dried cherries to this one, but really, you can get as creative as you want and the results will always be great. Try cranberries instead of cherries, for example. Or for a mocha-java version, add 1 teaspoon instant espresso powder along with the flour; and for an orange-chocolate version, add 1 teaspoon grated orange zest and 1 teaspoon orange extract (in place of the vanilla) and omit the dried fruit. Play around to find what you like and make it your own unique creation!

½ pound (2 sticks) + 3 tablespoons
  cold unsalted butter, cubed
1½ cups sugar
5 large eggs
2 large egg yolks
2½ teaspoons vanilla extract
2½ cups all-purpose flour, plus more
  for shaping

½ cup unsweetened cocoa powder,
  sifted
2½ teaspoons baking powder
¾ teaspoon kosher salt
½ cup dried cherries
1 cup semisweet chocolate chips

Preheat the oven to 350°F. Line a 10 x 15-inch baking sheet with parchment paper or a nonstick silicone liner.

In a stand mixer fitted with the paddle attachment, cream the butter and sugar on medium speed until light and fluffy. Reduce the speed to low and beat in the whole eggs, egg yolks, and vanilla, making sure they are incorporated fully. In a bowl, whisk together the flour, cocoa, baking powder, and salt. Beat the flour mixture into the dough on medium speed, then beat in the cherries and chocolate chips.

To achieve that famous biscotti shape, divide the dough into two portions

(continued on page 134)

and roll each into a log about the length of the baking sheet. It's okay to use more flour on the surface to help shape the logs, as the dough will be sticky. Place the logs on the baking sheet and gently pat down the tops of the logs to square them off.

Bake for 10 minutes, then rotate the pan front to back and bake for 15 minutes more. Take the pan out of the oven; leave the oven on but turn the temperature down to 325°F. Allow the logs to cool slightly, still on the pan.

Slice the logs crosswise into ¾-inch-thick slices and lay them flat on the baking sheet. Bake for 6 minutes. Flip the biscotti over and bake 6 minutes longer. Transfer to wire racks to cool.

chef it up!

Melt dark or white chocolate chips with vegetable shortening (this gives the chocolate a glossy effect). Use 1 teaspoon shortening per cup of white chocolate and 2 teaspoons per cup of dark. Dip one end of the finished biscotti into the melted chocolate.

BROWN BUTTER PIZZELLE

MAKES ABOUT 16 PIZZELLE

Pizzelle are Italian cookies from the Abruzzo region. Resembling crisp, thin waffles, pizzelle are traditionally made in a cast-iron mold directly over an open flame. With today's technology you can make pizzelle in an electric pizzelle iron, which cuts the cooking time in half (and avoids the need for an open flame). With their snowflake-like appearance, these tasty cookies are perfect as a garnish for ice cream. **SPECIAL EQUIPMENT:** pizzelle iron

¼ pound (1 stick) unsalted butter
3 large eggs
¾ cup sugar
1 teaspoon vanilla extract

⅛ teaspoon ground aniseed
1¾ cups all-purpose flour
2 teaspoons baking powder

In a small saucepan, melt the butter over medium heat. After the outer edge of the butter starts to turn brown, continue to cook for 2 minutes. Take the butter off the heat and allow it to completely cool in the pot.

In a large bowl, whisk together the eggs, sugar, and browned butter. Whisk in the vanilla, aniseed, flour, and baking powder until smooth.

Preheat a pizzelle iron according to the manufacturer's directions. Spoon the batter onto the iron and cook as directed.

chef it up!

When the cookie is still warm and flexible, right out of the iron, I wrap it around a cannoli form, a metal tube about 5 inches long and 1 inch in diameter. (Most pizzelle irons come with cannoli forms.) Then I stuff the shell with cannoli cream, made with a mixture of *impastata* (drained and pressed ricotta cheese), sugar, heavy cream, orange zest, and lemon zest.

FONTINA PUFFS

MAKES ABOUT 30 PUFFS

When diners come into a busy New York City restaurant, it's often customary to present them with what is known as an *amuse bouche* or a small bite. This freebie is typically given at the beginning of the meal when the guests have been seated, but I wanted to offer something as well to those still standing, waiting for their tables to be ready. I developed these Fontina puffs as an Italian take on the French *gougère*, which is a savory cream puff made with cheese. My staff jokingly referred to them as "cheesy poofs," but all kidding aside, they were a hit with those guests waiting to begin their evening of dining. At home when I make these, I use them as an appetizer and everyone eats them like candy. Warning: These can be addictive! **SPECIAL EQUIPMENT:** pastry bag, #8 plain tip

1½ cups water
1½ tablespoons kosher salt
2 teaspoons ground white pepper
   (black is okay, too)
12 tablespoons (1½ sticks) unsalted
   butter

1 cup all-purpose flour
7 large eggs
¾ cup shredded Fontina cheese (about
   3 ounces)

Preheat the oven to 375°F. Line a baking sheet with parchment paper (see "Batch Baking," opposite page).

In a medium, deep pot, combine the water, salt, pepper, and butter. Bring to a boil. Reduce the heat to low and add the flour all at once, stirring until the mixture forms a dough. I strongly suggest using a wooden spoon for this step. Continue to stir the dough over low heat for 1½ minutes to help dry the dough out a bit. This is what starts to form the texture of the puff. When the dough starts to stick and form a slight skin on the bottom of the pot, take it off the heat.

Transfer the hot dough to a stand mixer fitted with the paddle attachment and beat the dough at medium speed for about 3 minutes or until the steam stops escaping the top. Reduce the speed to low, add the eggs one at a time and beat well after each addition until fully incorporated into the dough. (The dough will break apart into pieces, but don't worry, it comes back together.) After all the eggs have been added, add the cheese and beat on medium speed for 1 minute more.

To make the puffs, fit a pastry bag with a #8 plain tip and scoop the dough into the pastry bag. Pipe 30 balls of dough onto the baking sheet, spacing them 1½ inches apart. Bake the puffs for 10 minutes. Reduce the oven temperature to 325°F, rotate the pan front to back, and bake until the puffs have risen and developed a slight crack on the top, with a pale brown coloring, about 10 minutes longer. Serve warm.

INSIDER TIP • BATCH BAKING

Most recipes for cookies and small pastries make more than can fit on a single baking sheet. Since many home cooks may only have one large baking sheet, the cookies or pastries need to be baked in batches (just be sure the pan cools in between batches). But if you have more than one baking sheet, you can bake 2 sheets at once. When you preheat the oven, place one rack in the top third of the oven and a second rack in the bottom third. Place a baking sheet on each rack. Halfway through the cooking time, switch the sheets from rack to rack, and at the same time, rotate the sheets from front to back for even browning.

LATTICE-TOP BLUEBERRY PIE

MAKES ONE 9-INCH PIE

When you make a pie filling using fruit, a common concern is whether the filling will be thick enough after it's baked, so as not to have a watery pie. A mixture of water and cornstarch, known as a "slurry," is the solution. Slurries are the most efficient way to ensure little leakage and the desired consistency.

Flour, for rolling the dough
Simple Pie Dough (page 41), chilled
3 tablespoons + 1 cup water

¼ cup cornstarch
6 tablespoons sugar
3½ cups blueberries

On a well-floured surface, start flattening and rolling out one of the disks of dough, turning it often to keep it round. (Leave the other disk refrigerated.) Continue to roll the dough until ⅛ inch thick and about 12 inches in diameter. Transfer the dough to a baking sheet and refrigerate until needed (this is for the lattice strips).

Roll out the second disk of dough in the same manner. Gently roll the dough onto the rolling pin. Position the dough over a 9-inch pie plate and carefully unroll the dough into the pan. Using your hands, gently press the dough into the bottom and up the sides of the pan. Leave the dough hanging over the pan edge all around. Trim the overhang to ½ inch.

Preheat the oven to 350°F.

In a bowl, whisk together 3 tablespoons of the water, the cornstarch, and 1 tablespoon of the sugar (this is the slurry).

In a medium saucepan, combine the remaining 1 cup water and remaining 5 tablespoons sugar. Bring to a boil. Whisk in the slurry, bring back to a boil, and cook for 1 minute to cook the raw taste out of the cornstarch. The mixture should go from opaque and runny to a clear gel-like consistency. Take off the

(continued on page 141)

heat and gently fold in the blueberries. Let the blueberry filling cool before pouring it into the bottom crust.

Remove the chilled dough from the refrigerator and cut into ten 1-inch-wide strips. Pour the berry mixture into the crust. Lay 5 strips of dough parallel to one another across the pie (putting the longer strips toward the middle and the shorter ones at the sides). Fold every other strip back halfway. Place a long strip in the center of the pie, perpendicular to the other strips. Unfold the folded strips back down over the perpendicular strip. Then fold back every other strip again, this time lifting up the strips that are underneath the perpendicular strip. Place another strip across the pie parallel to the perpendicular strip. Continue this process until you reach one edge of the pie, then repeat the process on the other side of the pie.

Trim the dough strips even with the rim of the pie. Fold the overhang in and crimp the edge of the pie.

Bake until the crust is golden brown, 40 to 50 minutes; rotate the pie plate front to back halfway through.

VARIATION

Strawberry-Chocolate Pie: Substitute quartered strawberries for the blueberries. Stir in ¾ cup semisweet chocolate chips once the cooked fruit mixture has completely cooled. You don't want the chocolate to melt.

HOT CROSS BUNS

MAKES 16 BUNS

This hot cross bun recipe comes from my Irish grandmother. The buns are proofed several times before baking, allowing the texture to be soft and airy. They are perfect for breakfast with a nice hot cup of coffee. **SPECIAL EQUIPMENT:** paper cornet (see "Make Your Own Cornet," page 74) or pastry bag and #2 plain tip (optional)

BUNS
½ cup whole milk
2 envelopes (¼ ounce each) active dry
  yeast (4½ teaspoons)
½ cup granulated sugar
1 teaspoon kosher salt
3¾ cups all-purpose flour, sifted, plus
  more for kneading
2 large eggs, beaten
¼ pound (1 stick) unsalted butter,
  melted and cooled
1 teaspoon ground cinnamon

½ cup dried currants
¼ cup finely diced citron
Cooking spray
Egg wash: 1 egg white beaten with
  1 tablespoon water

ICING
½ cup confectioners' sugar
1 tablespoon whole milk
1 teaspoon light corn syrup
¼ teaspoon vanilla extract
Small pinch of kosher salt

MAKE THE BUNS: In a small saucepan or in the microwave, heat the milk just until it's warm. It should only just be warm, *not hot*, and it should definitely not come to a boil.

Transfer the warmed milk to the bowl of a stand mixer fitted with the paddle attachment. Add the yeast, sugar, and salt. Let the mixture sit for 5 minutes.

With the mixer on low speed, mix in one-third of the flour, followed by the eggs. Mix in the melted butter, cinnamon, and the remaining two-thirds of the flour. Beat in the currants and citron. Coat a large bowl with cooking spray and transfer the dough to it. Cover with a damp towel and let rise in a warm place until doubled in bulk, about 1½ hours.

Punch down the dough. Turn it out onto a floured surface and knead by hand for 1 minute. Return it to the greased bowl, cover again, and place in the refrigerator to slowly rise again for 2½ hours.

Coat the bottom and sides of a 9 x 13-inch baking pan with cooking spray. Punch down the dough and turn it out onto a floured surface. Cut it into 4 portions. Cut each of the portions into quarters, creating 16 buns. Gently roll them into rounds. Place the buns in the greased baking pan in 4 rows of 4. Brush the tops of the buns with the egg wash. Cover with a towel and let the buns rise again at room temperature until doubled in size, about 1 hour. The buns will touch.

While the buns are rising, preheat the oven to 350°F.

Bake the buns until golden brown, about 20 minutes. Let the buns cool in the pan.

MAKE THE ICING: In a small bowl, whisk together the confectioners' sugar, milk, corn syrup, vanilla, and salt until smooth.

When the buns are cool, dip a knife in the icing (or fill a cornet or a pastry bag fitted with a #2 plain tip with the icing) and draw a continuous line of icing across the tops of all the buns down the rows in one direction. Then turn the pan and make perpendicular lines of icing across the rows in the other directions to make the traditional icing "cross" on each bun.

BEAVER TAILS

MAKES 12 PASTRIES

When I was pregnant with my son, my husband and I took a trip to Montreal, Canada, for a small getaway before the baby came. Being a chef and pregnant, for me this trip was mostly about food—and spending time with my husband, of course. I was hungry so constantly that I could swear I was going to give birth to a 20-pound baby. So it was important that I plot out the food scene on this trip. In my research for restaurants, I came across a lot of people mentioning beaver tails, a fried yeast dough with various toppings, served hot. I just had to get my hands on one. Sure, the fact that the dough is stretched and flattened out to be the shape of a beaver tail is cute, but it's the actual dough here that is so special and tasty. I tracked down a beaver tail in a mall, of all places, and was hooked immediately. It might even have been a lunch substitute for me one day, but that was the baby's fault, not mine.

SPECIAL EQUIPMENT: deep-frying thermometer or a deep fryer; spider

½ cup warm (108° to 110°F) water
5 teaspoons active dry yeast
1⅓ cups + 1 teaspoon sugar
1 cup whole milk
2 teaspoons kosher salt
1 tablespoon vanilla extract
2 large eggs, at room temperature

3 cups all-purpose flour, plus more for rolling
1½ cups whole wheat flour
⅓ cup grapeseed or vegetable oil
Cooking spray
1 tablespoon ground cinnamon
Vegetable oil, for deep-frying

In the bowl of a stand mixer, whisk together the warm water, yeast, and 1 teaspoon of the sugar by hand. Let stand for 3 to 5 minutes for the yeast to start to activate.

While the yeast is activating, in a small saucepan or in the microwave, warm the milk.

Place the bowl with the yeast in it on the mixer fitted with the dough hook

(continued on page 146)

and mix in the warm milk, ⅓ cup of the sugar, the salt, vanilla, and eggs on low speed. Add the flours and grapeseed oil and continue to mix on low speed until the dough comes together and pulls away from the sides of the bowl.

Coat a large bowl with cooking spray and transfer the dough to it. Cover with plastic or a kitchen towel and let rise in a warm place until doubled in bulk, about 2 hours.

Punch down the dough. Divide the dough in half, then divide each half into 6 portions. Roll each portion into an oval ball about the size and shape of an egg. On a lightly floured surface, flatten each ball of dough and pull it slightly to elongate, like a beaver tail, about 5 inches long and ¼ inch thick.

In a large bowl, whisk together the remaining 1 cup sugar and the cinnamon; keep at hand.

In a heavy-bottomed, deep saucepan, pour in enough vegetable oil to come up 3 inches (or use a deep fryer, if you have one). Heat the oil to 350°F. Line one or two baking sheets with paper towels.

Working in batches, gently drop 2 beaver tails at a time into the oil. Fry until golden brown, about 4 minutes. Remove with a spider and drain the tails on paper towels. Toss in the cinnamon sugar. Serve warm.

CHRUSTIKI

MAKES ABOUT 30 PIECES

This recipe comes from my great-grandmother on my Polish side, whom we called "Babcia." My favorite part about going to Babcia's house for Christmas was that she would make these amazing cookies and let me help her douse them in the confectioners' sugar before everyone devoured them. I was so lucky to even know a great-grandmother, let alone be able to bake with one. I've adapted the recipe a little by using a stand mixer instead of making the dough entirely by hand; the end result is just as good as I remember.

SPECIAL EQUIPMENT: pizza cutter (optional); spider

2½ cups all-purpose flour, plus more for kneading and rolling
1 teaspoon baking powder
¼ teaspoon kosher salt
7 large egg yolks

1 teaspoon vanilla extract
1 teaspoon confectioners' sugar, plus more for dusting
3 heaping tablespoons sour cream
Vegetable oil, for deep-frying

Sift the flour, baking powder, and salt together into a medium bowl.

In a stand mixer fitted with the paddle attachment, beat the egg yolks on low to medium speed until frothy. Beat in the vanilla, sugar, and sour cream. Blend the mixture well, then beat in the flour mixture.

Turn out the loose dough onto a floured work surface and lightly knead it until it becomes smooth and elastic, about 5 minutes. If the dough sticks to the work surface, knead in a little more flour. Divide the dough into 3 equal portions.

On a lightly floured surface, roll out the dough, one piece at a time, into a rough rectangle, making it as thin as you can, but without making it see-through. Keep the remaining dough covered with a moist towel while it waits.

(continued on page 148)

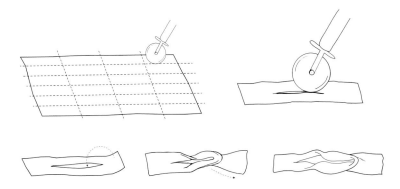

Cut the rolled-out dough into strips 3 to 4 inches long and 1½ inches wide. A pizza cutter works great for this, but you can use a knife. Slit each piece in the center. Pull one end through the slit so it has a sort of bow-tie look. As you work, place the cookies on a baking sheet and cover with a moist paper towel so they don't dry out.

Line one or more baking sheets with dry paper towels. In a heavy-bottomed, deep saucepan, pour in enough vegetable oil to come up 3 inches (or use a deep fryer if you have one). Heat the oil to 375°F. Working in batches, drop about 5 pieces of dough into the oil and fry until light golden, about 1½ minutes, turning over once. Remove the chrustiki with a spider and drain on the paper towels. Let cool. When cool, sift confectioners' sugar over them.

CHOCOLATE TORRONE

MAKES 1½ POUNDS

This recipe comes from my Italian great-grandmother. This traditional Italian Christmas candy is made by spreading it out between two sheets of an unleavened wheat wafer called *ostia*. However, I just use two non-stick silicone liners. **SPECIAL EQUIPMENT:** candy thermometer

1¼ pounds blanched hazelnuts
1 cup honey
1 cup + 1 tablespoon sugar
4 tablespoons water

2 large egg whites
1¾ cups unsweetened cocoa powder, sifted

Preheat the oven to 350°F. Spread out the hazelnuts on a baking sheet and bake until toasted, 8 to 10 minutes. Transfer the nuts to a plate to cool.

Line a 10 x 15-inch rimmed baking sheet with a nonstick silicone liner.

In a small saucepan, combine the honey, 1 cup of the sugar, and 2 tablespoons of the water. Bring to a boil. Continue to cook the syrup over medium heat until the temperature reaches 320°F.

While the honey syrup is boiling, in a stand mixer fitted with the whisk attachment, start to whip the egg whites on low speed.

When the honey syrup reaches 320°F, stream it down the side of the bowl (not onto the whisk) into the whites with the mixer running at low speed. Increase the speed to high and continue to whip the egg whites to stiff peaks.

In another saucepan, stir together the cocoa, the remaining 1 tablespoon sugar, and the remaining 2 tablespoons water over medium heat until creamy.

With the mixer running at medium speed, beat the cocoa mixture into the egg whites. Beat in the hazelnuts.

Pour the torrone into the pan and top with a second nonstick liner. Press it out with your hands until it looks even. Let cool, then cut into rectangles with a serrated knife. Store at room temperature.

Passion Fruit Pâte de Fruit

MAKES ABOUT THIRTY-SIX 1-INCH CUBES

I n the restaurant, I always have the guests end their meal with some small takeaway treat. This lovely fruit candy is so beautiful with its jewel-like appearance. The best part about this recipe is that the fruit juices and purees are interchangeable. As a pastry chef who values seasonality, I appreciate how much fun it is to change up the flavors when new fruits come in, and come up with delicious variations. **SPECIAL EQUIPMENT:** candy thermometer

Vegetable oil or cooking spray, for
   greasing the pan
6 tablespoons + 3¼ cups sugar, plus
   ½ cup for coating
1½ tablespoons powdered pectin

2½ cups passion fruit puree
½ cup glucose (available in baking
   supply stores)
2 teaspoons lemon juice
2 teaspoons water

Coat a 9 x 13-inch baking pan with vegetable oil.

In a small bowl, combine the 6 tablespoons sugar with the pectin. In a small saucepan, bring the passion fruit puree to a boil. Whisk the pectin-sugar mixture into the puree and bring the mixture back to a boil over medium heat, whisking constantly. Adding about 1 cup at a time, slowly whisk in the 3¼ cups sugar, stirring well after each addition and continuing to boil. Add the glucose and whisk, bringing again to a boil. Let simmer for 30 to 40 minutes, until it reaches 230°F. The mixture will be thick and the boiling bubbles will become large and slow-moving.

Take the mixture off the heat and stir in the lemon juice and water. Pour onto the oiled pan and let cool until it reaches room temperature.

Spread the ½ cup sugar on a work surface. Loosen the edges of the jelly with a small knife. Invert the pan and release the jelly onto the sugared surface. Cut the pâte de fruit into small squares and roll around in the sugar. You could also use little cutters to cut out fun shapes (dip the cutter in sugar as you work so it won't stick).

Store in an airtight container.

PEANUT BRITTLE

MAKES ABOUT 2½ POUNDS

Peanut brittle is an old-time candy that makes a wonderful hostess gift or take-home-from-dinner gift. Once you understand the basic structure of the recipe, you can get creative. See the variation below for an easy swap-out, then take the idea and run with it. **SPECIAL EQUIPMENT:** candy thermometer

Cooking spray, for greasing the pans
2 cups sugar
1 cup light corn syrup
1 cup water
2 teaspoons vanilla extract

2 cups raw blanched peanuts
1 tablespoon unsalted butter
1½ teaspoons baking soda
Pinch of salt
1 teaspoon light honey, such as acacia

Line a baking sheet with foil and coat with cooking spray. Set aside.

In a large, high-sided pot, stir together the sugar, corn syrup, water, and vanilla just to combine. Bring up to a bubble over high heat and cook, without stirring, until the syrup reaches 240°F. Add the peanuts and cook, stirring constantly, until the syrup reaches 300°F. Add the butter and baking soda and stir to combine. The mixture will bubble up and be hot, so stir carefully. Continue stirring until it foams up and is golden brown, about 10 seconds. Stir in the salt and honey.

Carefully pour the mixture onto the prepared baking sheet and let sit at room temperature until cooled and hardened, about 1 hour.

Break into smaller pieces and store at room temperature in an airtight container for up to 1 week.

VARIATION

Hawaiian Brittle: Replace the peanuts with macadamia nuts and add ¼ cup unsweetened shredded coconut when you stir in the nuts.

Showstoppers

This chapter focuses on presentation and desserts that are sure to wow your guests. The techniques used in this chapter are a bit more elevated in difficulty, but I've plotted them out step by step so they're simple to follow. You'll learn about classic French cakes as well as elegant flavor profiles that are sure to please everyone. I also let you in on a few secret recipes of a restaurant pastry chef that are so easy to adopt at home you'll wonder what all the fuss was about (see "Fancy-Looking Restaurant Foam," page 165).

St. Honoré Cake, page 173

PISTACHIO CUPCAKES
WITH MEYER LEMON FROSTING

MAKES 12 CUPCAKES

Cupcakes seem to be all the rage lately. I myself just can't get enough of them. The whimsical allowance you have when making cupcakes is celebrated in my kitchen. I find the more colorful they are, the better. Not only are they fun and fun to eat, they can really make a statement as part of the décor for a party. This recipe is one of my favorites because it's elegant and refined in flavor but packs a whole lot of fun in appearance. **SPECIAL EQUIPMENT:** pastry bag, #8 plain tip (optional)

CUPCAKES
2 cups cake flour
1 cup granulated sugar
½ cup unsalted pistachios, ground (see "Nut Flours" page 29)
½ teaspoon baking powder
½ teaspoon baking soda
½ teaspoon kosher salt
12 tablespoons (1½ sticks) unsalted butter, at room temperature
¾ cup sour cream
2 large eggs

1 tablespoon canola oil
1 teaspoon vanilla extract
2 teaspoons grated Meyer lemon zest
Green food coloring (optional)

FROSTING
1 package (8 ounces) cream cheese, at room temperature
½ cup confectioners' sugar
½ teaspoon vanilla extract
Grated zest and juice of 1 Meyer lemon

MAKE THE CUPCAKES: Preheat the oven to 350°F. Line 12 cups of a muffin tin with paper liners.

In a stand mixer fitted with the paddle attachment, mix the flour, granulated sugar, ground pistachios, baking powder, baking soda, and salt on low speed to combine. Add the butter and sour cream and mix until well combined. Add the eggs one at a time, beating well after each addition. Beat in the oil, vanilla,

(continued on page 158)

lemon zest, and food coloring (if using). Beat on medium speed for about 45 seconds. Stop the mixer and scrape the bowl down periodically with a rubber spatula to make sure everything is well combined.

Divide the batter among the muffin cups. Bake until the cupcakes spring back to the touch and a cake tester comes out clean, 16 to 20 minutes. Let the cupcakes cool in the pan before frosting.

MAKE THE FROSTING: In a stand mixer fitted with the paddle attachment, cream the cream cheese with the confectioners' sugar until light and smooth. Stop the mixer and scrape down the bowl with a rubber spatula to incorporate all the cream cheese and cream it well. Beat in the vanilla, lemon zest, and lemon juice. Continue to beat on medium-high speed until the frosting is smooth and creamy.

After the cupcakes have cooled, use either a pastry bag fitted with a #8 plain tip or a small offset spatula to apply the frosting to the cakes. The cupcakes will keep in an airtight container for up to 5 days.

chef it up!

I could never send a bare cupcake to the table. It's got to have a little garnish on top. The easiest thing to do is to sprinkle some ground pistachios and a little grated lemon zest on top. But I also like to top the cupcakes with teeny pieces of candied lemon (see photo, page 156).

How to Properly Cut a Layer Cake

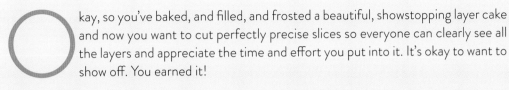

Okay, so you've baked, and filled, and frosted a beautiful, showstopping layer cake and now you want to cut perfectly precise slices so everyone can clearly see all the layers and appreciate the time and effort you put into it. It's okay to want to show off. You earned it!

SET UP

1. Fill a tall cup or container with hot water. Tap water is fine, but the hotter the better.
2. Select a knife. A long slicing knife is preferable, but if you don't have one, no worries. Try to pick a knife that's got a clean, straight edge. Never use a serrated knife (except for angel food cakes).
3. Have a clean towel, either paper or cloth, at the ready.

THE CUT

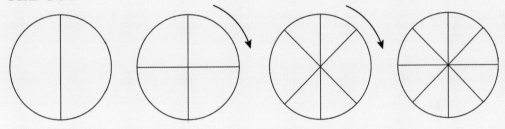

1. Dip your knife in the hot water to heat it up and wipe off the excess water on the towel. Make your first cut straight across, cutting the cake evenly in half.
2. Turn the cake 90 degrees and repeat step 1 to cut the cake into 4 quarters
3. Heat your knife again and cut each quarter in half again making 8 equal slices. Continue with this process, dividing each segment in half, until you've gotten the number of slices you need.
4. Use a cake server to lift out each piece and transfer to cake plates.

NOTE: For large square cakes, cut the whole cake in half in one direction, then turn the pan and cut the cake in half in the other direction (perpendicular). Now, cutting all the way across the cake, continue subdividing the sections in half until you get the total number of slices you're looking for. The object is to get nice, even slices.

CHOCOLATE HAZELNUT CAKE

SERVES 12 TO 16

This cake is pure decadence. It's a chocolate lover's dream cake. The classic flavor profile of hazelnut and chocolate makes the cake as delicious as it is as elegant. **SPECIAL EQUIPMENT:** 9-inch round cardboard cake circle, pastry brush, pastry bag, #8 star tip, small offset spatula

1 cup skin-on hazelnuts
¼ cup granulated sugar
¼ cup water
1 tablespoon Frangelico or other
    hazelnut liqueur

Basic Chocolate Cake (page 18), baked
    and cooled
2 recipes Ganache Filling (page 75);
    see Note

Preheat the oven to 350°F.

Spread out the hazelnuts in an even layer on a rimmed baking sheet and bake until toasted, 5 to 10 minutes. Transfer the nuts to a plate to cool, so they don't continue cooking from carryover cooking. When they're cool enough to handle, roughly chop or crush the hazelnuts.

In a small saucepan, combine the sugar, water, and Frangelico. Bring to a boil to dissolve the sugar. Let the syrup cool to just warm or room temperature.

Place one cake layer on top of a 9-inch round cardboard cake circle. Using a pastry brush, brush the entire surface of the cake layer with the syrup until it feels moist to the touch, letting it soak in (you may not need all the syrup). Spread the cake with ganache about ½ inch thick and top with the second cake layer. Spread the top and sides with a thin layer of the ganache until smooth. Fit a pastry bag with a #8 star tip, fill the bag with the remaining ganache, and pipe rosettes (see "Decorating with Icing," page 73) around the entire cake. Top with the toasted hazelnuts.

NOTE: If you want to skip the rosette decoration, you'll only need 1 recipe of Ganache Filling.

RED VELVET MACARONS

MAKES 24 MACARONS

The French *macaron* seems to have had a revival recently. Once only seen at old-school French patisseries or weddings, they've made a comeback, becoming one of the hottest dessert trends in America. The delicate meringue and almond cookie is seen everywhere in various flavors and colors and is often used to give as a gift or add to the décor of an event. Technique is important when making a macaron, so here is my variation on the popular cookie with some tips to help you along the way. **SPECIAL EQUIPMENT:** 2 pastry bags, #4 plain tip

1 cup confectioners' sugar
1 cup almond meal/flour
¼ teaspoon kosher salt
2 large egg whites
¼ cup granulated sugar

1½ teaspoons unsweetened cocoa
    powder, sifted
1 bottle (¼ ounce) red food coloring
½ recipe Cream Cheese Frosting (page
    67)

In a food processer, combine the confectioners' sugar, almond meal, and salt and process until finely ground. Sift the mixture into a large bowl, discarding any lumps or unground almond meal.

In a stand mixer fitted with the whisk attachment, whip the egg whites on medium speed to medium peaks while slowly adding the granulated sugar. The sugar will stabilize the whites.

Sprinkle a small amount of the ground almond mixture over the meringue and gently fold it in with a rubber spatula. Add the meringue to the remaining almond mixture and gently fold in with the spatula until well combined. Fold in the cocoa powder and food coloring.

Preheat the oven to 325°F. Line a 10 x 15-inch rimmed baking sheet with parchment paper or a nonstick silicone liner.

Fit a pastry bag with a #4 plain tip and spoon in the batter. Pipe 1-inch rounds

(continued on page 164)

of batter on the baking sheet, spacing them 2 inches apart. (You'll get about 16 cookies per baking sheet. If you have a second baking sheet, line it and pipe more cookies. Otherwise bake them in three batches for a total of 48.) Let each sheet of cookies air-dry for 30 minutes before baking, to form a slight skin on top, so they will rise and form the characteristic "foot" when baked.

Bake the cookies until they have puffed up a little and look dry on top, 10 to 20 minutes. Let the cookies cool for 2 to 3 minutes on the baking sheet, then transfer to a wire rack.

To assemble the macarons, carefully flip the cookies over on the baking sheet so the bottoms are facing up. Fit a clean pastry bag with a #4 plain tip and fill with the frosting. Pipe frosting right out to the edge of the cookie on every other row of cookies. Top with an unfrosted cookie, flat side down. Serve right away or store in an airtight container for up to 1 week. (These freeze well, already filled and all. Wrap the container in plastic wrap to avoid ice crystals. Take the container out of the freezer and let it thaw in the refrigerator overnight before serving.)

INSIDER TIP • TANT POUR TANT
Macarons always start with what the French call *tant pour tant*, meaning equal parts (by weight) of almond meal and confectioners' sugar.

Fancy-Looking Restaurant Foam

MAKES ABOUT 30 GOOD SQUEEZES OF FOAM

When you're a pastry chef in a competitive industry, you have to keep up with all the latest trends. Foams, or *espumas*, are all the rage right now and quickly turning into a staple element in the fine dining experience. But I'll bet you won't believe how stupid-easy it is to make one of those stunning foams. It's all thanks to a little tool called a siphon (the most common brand you'll find is called an iSi Whip), which is a dispenser that whips cream using CO_2 chargers—much like its well-known relative, Reddi-wip. These dispensers (and replacement chargers) can be found in almost every kitchen store these days, as well as online. The possibilities are endless for what you can whip up with this tool, everything from a pomegranate foam for a sorbet to an airy savory mousse to top a creamy pea soup. You can be as creative as you want.

2 tablespoons + 1 teaspoon unflavored powdered gelatin
¾ cup cold water

2 cups fruit juice
¼ cup sugar

In a small bowl, sprinkle the gelatin over the water. Set aside to soften.

In a medium saucepan, combine the fruit juice and sugar. Bring to a boil. Take it off the heat and add the softened gelatin, stirring until dissolved. Let the mixture cool to room temperature. (Do not refrigerate; it needs to stay a liquid.)

Pour the juice mixture into the canister of the dispenser and charge it three times, shaking it up between charges. Squeeze out the foam and enjoy!

NOTE: Unless you're serving a giant crowd, you won't use the full canister of foam. But the liquid can easily be saved and used again. Pour it out of the canister into a container, cover, and refrigerate. The liquid will gel when it's cold, so to reuse it you have to very gently melt it on the stovetop or in the microwave. Pour the melted juice into the canister of the dispenser, recharge it, and you're good to go again.

PERSIMMON PUDDING IN A JAR

One of the restaurants that I used to work at had a "cheesecake in a jar" as their signature dessert. I couldn't ever take it off menu because it was so popular, but I always felt the jar had many other possibilities for baked goods, since it was so cute in its presentation. For Christmas Eve I developed this Persimmon Pudding in a Jar. I served it right in the jars, still a little warm with a dollop of some Brandied Whipped Cream (page 80; make only ½ recipe). I find it perfect for a late fall or winter dessert.

2 or 3 ripe Fuyu persimmons (enough to make 1 cup pulp)
1½ teaspoons baking soda
¼ cup stout (such as Guinness)
½ pound (2 sticks) unsalted butter, at room temperature
1 cup + 6 tablespoons packed light brown sugar

5 large eggs
1 tablespoon vanilla extract
1⅓ cups all-purpose flour
¼ cup unsweetened cocoa powder, sifted
½ teaspoon ground cinnamon
⅛ teaspoon ground ginger
Pinch of kosher salt

Preheat the oven to 350°F.

Peel and seed the persimmons and cut the flesh into large chunks. In a saucepan, combine the persimmons and enough water to just cover. Bring to a boil and cook until the persimmons are soft and tender.

Drain well and transfer the persimmon flesh to a blender. Puree, adding a little water to get the persimmon moving in the blender. Measure out 1 cup of the puree, transfer to a small bowl, and whisk in the baking soda and stout. Set aside.

In a stand mixer fitted with the whisk attachment, cream the butter and brown sugar on low speed. Add the eggs one at a time, beating well after each addition. Beat in the vanilla. Make sure to stop and scrape down the bowl with a

(continued on page 168)

rubber spatula as you go so that there are no lumps. On medium speed, beat in the persimmon mixture. Beat in the flour, cocoa, cinnamon, ginger, and salt.

Divide the batter among six 4- to 5-ounce canning jars, filling each three-fourths of the way up.

Place the jars in a roasting pan, making sure the jars are not touching one another. Fill the pan one-fourth of the way up with hot water. Cover the entire pan with foil, making sure to leave headspace above the tops of the jars because the puddings will rise. Bake until the puddings have risen and spring back to the touch, and a cake tester comes out clean, 25 to 35 minutes. Uncover the roasting pan and transfer the jars to a wire rack to cool.

Serve warm in the jar (with whipped cream, if desired).

VARIATIONS
Zucchini Pudding in a Jar: Replace the persimmons with zucchini and cook as directed; you need enough zucchini to get 1¼ cups pulp (cook more than you need to be safe). Omit the stout. Omit the cocoa powder. Increase the flour to 1⅓ cups + ¼ cup.
Mango Pudding in a Jar: Replace the persimmons with mango and cook as directed; you need enough mango to get 1¼ cups pulp (cook more than you need to be safe). Omit the stout. Omit the cocoa powder, cinnamon, and ginger. Increase the flour to 1⅓ cups + ¼ cup.
Eggplant Pudding in a Jar: (Yes, eggplant.) Replace the persimmons with eggplant and cook as directed; you need enough eggplant to get 1¼ cups pulp (cook more than you need to be safe). Omit the stout. Omit the cinnamon and ginger.

CANNELLES

MAKES 24 CANNELLES

There are probably only a few foods in your life that you vividly remember falling in love with in an instant, appreciating their simple genius at first bite. For me, that's the cannelle (or *cannelé* in French). This sweet little pastry was said to have been created by nuns in Bordeaux almost 200 years ago. Well, if French nuns can cook this well, I wouldn't mind visiting the convent every once in a while for some lessons. The crispy caramelized outside against the creamy, almost custardlike inside is a perfect pairing. **SPECIAL EQUIPMENT:** 24 small (1½-inch) copper cannelle molds (see page 198)

3⅓ cups whole milk
2 large eggs
1 large egg yolk
1 vanilla bean, split lengthwise
4 tablespoons (½ stick) unsalted
   butter, melted and cooled to room
   temperature

2 tablespoons dark rum
2 tablespoons sugar
1¼ cups all-purpose flour
Pinch of kosher salt
Melted butter and cooking spray, for
   greasing the molds

In a bowl, combine the milk, whole eggs, and egg yolk. Scrape in the vanilla seeds. Stir to blend. Stir in the melted butter, rum, and sugar. Add the flour and salt, and with a hand blender, beat to just incorporate them into the batter. Cover the batter with plastic wrap and refrigerate overnight.

Preheat the oven to 400°F.

Brush 24 small (1½-inch-deep) cannelle molds heavily with melted butter, then coat liberally with cooking spray. (The molds need a lot of grease; don't be shy.) Whisk the batter to reblend and transfer to a measuring cup or pitcher with a spout. Put the molds on a baking sheet and pour in the batter almost to the top. Bake for 16 minutes. Turn the oven down to 350°F and bake an additional 25 minutes. When the tops are dark brown, they are done. Allow to cool in the molds before turning them out. Store airtight at room temperature.

MACADAMIA–KEY LIME CHEESECAKE

SERVES 12 TO 14

Cheesecakes are often thought of as dense and heavy, but this riff is light and refreshing. The fresh citrus flavors are perfectly complemented by the macadamia nut crust. The addition of the sweetened condensed milk helps offset the sour and bitter flavor of a Key lime; it's a good trick to use when baking with sour flavors.

CRUST
Cooking spray
1¾ cups graham cracker crumbs
½ cup ground macadamia nuts (see "Nut Flours," page 29)
Pinch of kosher salt
5 tablespoons unsalted butter, melted, plus more for the pan

FILLING
4 packages (8 ounces each) cream cheese, at room temperature
2 cups sugar
5 large eggs, at room temperature
¾ cup sour cream, at room temperature

¼ cup heavy cream, at room temperature
1 can (14 ounces) sweetened condensed milk
¼ cup fresh Key lime juice (this could take as many as 20 limes, if they're very small)
2 tablespoons all-purpose flour
1 teaspoon vanilla extract

TOPPING
1¾ cups sour cream
¼ cup sugar
1 teaspoon vanilla extract
Grated zest of 2 regular limes

MAKE THE CRUST: Preheat the oven to 325°F. Line the bottom of a 10-inch springform pan with a round of parchment paper and coat the paper with cooking spray. Wrap the outside of the pan with foil, taking care to cover the seam at the bottom. (The pan is going into a water bath and you don't want any water to get in.)

(continued on page 172)

In a bowl, blend together the graham cracker crumbs, macadamias, and salt. Add the melted butter and stir to thoroughly combine. Press the crumb mixture into the bottom and ½ to 1 inch up the sides of the springform pan.

Bake the crust for 10 minutes to set. Remove from the oven but leave the oven on. Let the crust cool completely.

MAKE THE FILLING: In a stand mixer fitted with the paddle attachment, beat together the cream cheese and sugar on medium speed until creamy, about 2 minutes. Reduce the speed to low and beat in the eggs, followed by the sour cream and heavy cream. Beat in the condensed milk, lime juice, flour, and vanilla. Scrape the bowl often.

Choose a roasting pan that will hold the springform pan and place the springform in the roasting pan. Place the roasting pan on a pulled-out oven rack. Pour the filling into the crust. Carefully pour hot water into the roasting pan (staying well away from the springform, so you don't get any water into the cheesecake batter) to come halfway up the sides of the springform pan. Gently slide the rack back into place and close the oven door.

Bake until the cheesecake is just set in the center, 1 hour to 1 hour 15 minutes.

MAKE THE TOPPING: In a small bowl, whisk together the sour cream, sugar, vanilla, and lime zest.

Remove the cheesecake from the water bath. Top the cheesecake with the sour cream and return it to the oven for 6 minutes to set the topping. Turn off the oven and leave the cheesecake inside to completely cool, about 6 hours. Cover and refrigerate for at least 1 hour.

Remove the pan sides and cut into slices.

chef it up!

For a restaurant-worthy presentation, I grind up some more graham crackers and gently press it into the sides of the cheesecake after baking.

ST. HONORÉ CAKE

SERVES 12 TO 14

I remember the first time I laid eyes on a *gâteau St-Honoré*. It was at my first pastry job at a small French pastry shop. I was sixteen and eager to learn everything I could about the classic French desserts they produced. The holidays were always the busiest for us, filled with longer hours, shirts stained with red and green buttercream, and the phone constantly ringing with orders. Everyone hustled to fill not only the pastry case, but also special cake orders, including the St. Honoré Cake. This French classic is cream puffs filled with vanilla pastry cream, dipped in caramel, and attached to a disk of puff pastry, and then the whole thing is filled with even more delicious cream—this cake blew my mind when I ate it. The technique that goes into this cake may seem complex, but I assure you it's well worth it for this genuine showstopper. **SPECIAL EQUIPMENT:** 2 pastry bags, #8 plain tip, #2 plain tip; additional pastry bag and #4 plain tip (optional, for piping whipped cream)

Pâte à Choux dough (page 48), unbaked
½ pound Shortcut Puff Pastry (page 50); see Note page 175
Granulated sugar, for rolling out the pastry
Vanilla Pastry Cream (page 77), cooled

CARAMEL
1 cup granulated sugar
3½ tablespoons water

WHIPPED CREAM
1 cup heavy cream, chilled
½ cup confectioners' sugar
1 vanilla bean, split lengthwise

Preheat the oven to 350°F. Line a baking sheet with parchment paper. Reserving about 1½ cups of the pâte à choux, fit a pastry bag with a #8 plain tip and fill the bag with the remaining dough. Pipe out 20 small puffs (you only need 16, but pipe extras in case some of them break when you fill them). Follow the basic recipe and bake according to the directions. Meanwhile, fill the

(continued on page 174)

same pastry bag with the reserved dough, close the bag at the top, roll it down, and set aside. (Keeping the pastry in the bag prevents it from forming a skin.)

If you don't already have the oven on from making the puffs, preheat the oven to 350°F. Line a baking sheet with parchment paper or a nonstick silicone liner.

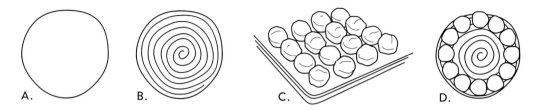

A.   B.   C.   D.

Sprinkle a work surface with granulated sugar. Roll out the puff pastry to about ⅛ inch thick. Cut out a 9-inch round of pastry **(A)** and place it on the baking sheet. Prick the pastry with a fork to prevent it from rising. Place a sheet of parchment paper over the pastry and invert another baking sheet on top to weight down the pastry. Bake for 15 minutes; the pastry will be only partially baked. Take it out of the oven and remove the top pan and parchment paper.

Using the reserved pâte à choux, pipe a spiral over the whole round of puff pastry **(B)**. Return it to the oven and bake until golden brown, 25 to 30 minutes.

Fit another pastry bag with a #2 plain tip and fill the bag with the pastry cream. Fill 16 of the puffs **(C)** with pastry cream. You won't use all the pastry cream for this step; more will get used later.

MAKE THE CARAMEL: Line a baking sheet with a nonstick silicone liner. In a small, heavy-bottomed saucepan, stir together the sugar and water and heat over medium heat until the mixture starts to turns a light amber color. Remove from the heat and swirl around (don't stir) until it has an even color. Put it back over the heat until it turns medium amber. Take the pan off the heat and carefully dip the top of each cream puff in the caramel. Place the cream puffs caramel-side down on the baking sheet to cool. This will make a caramel "foot" on the puff (see photo, page 155) for a prettier presentation. Once the caramel on the cream puffs has set, spoon a small amount of caramel on the plain side of each puff to use as the glue, and fasten the puffs onto the outer edge of the circle of puff and choux **(D)**, using as many as will fit (there may be 1 or 2 extra). (**NOTE:** If the caramel starts to get too hard and sets while you're working with it, place it back over heat briefly just to remelt it.) The cake will now resemble a crown.

Fill the center with the remaining pastry cream.

MAKE THE WHIPPED CREAM: In a stand mixer fitted with the whisk attachment, start whipping the cream on low speed. When the cream just begins to gain volume, slowly add the sugar and scrape in the vanilla seeds. (Save the vanilla bean halves for another use; see page 67.) Continue to whip on medium speed until stiff peaks form. Spread the whipped cream over the top of the cake. (Or fit a pastry bag with a #4 plain tip, fill the bag with the whipped cream, and pipe it over the top.) Let the cake set in the refrigerator for at least 1 hour before serving.

NOTE: Make the full recipe of the puff pastry, measure out what you need for this recipe (about one-fourth of the total), and freeze the remaining pastry for another use. (Shhhhh! Don't tell anyone I said so, but it's okay to use store-bought frozen all-butter puff pastry, if you want. You'll need a single sheet of puff pastry.)

chef it up!

I know you must be thinking to yourselves, "Really? There's something fancier than the recipe I just read?" And the answer is yes. When I really want to go all out with a St. Honoré Cake, I top it with a caramel cage. But that's graduate-level pastry stuff. You'll have to wait for my next book to learn how to do that.

BOURBON-CHOCOLATE PECAN PIE

MAKES ONE 9-INCH PIE

Every Thanksgiving I do what I call my "Great Pie Bake." Not only do I usually have to bake about 50 pies for whatever restaurant I'm working at, but I'm always chugging coffee at ten o'clock the night before my family's dinner so I can squeeze in baking a few pies for that, too. A pastry chef's job is never done! One year, when I was bored with straight-up pecan pie, I added chocolate and bourbon. Who doesn't love the gooey factor that chocolate gives to a pecan pie?

Flour, for rolling the dough
½ recipe Simple Pie Dough (page 41), chilled
1½ cups granulated sugar
¾ cup light corn syrup
4 tablespoons (½ stick) unsalted butter, melted
6 tablespoons bourbon
6 large eggs, lightly beaten
1 heaping cup semisweet chocolate chips

1½ cups whole pecan halves
1½ cups pecan pieces or chopped pecans

BROWN SUGAR CRÈME FRAÎCHE
¾ cup crème fraîche
¼ cup heavy cream
2 tablespoons light brown sugar, sifted to remove lumps
1 tablespoon confectioners' sugar
1 teaspoon vanilla extract

On a well-floured surface, start flattening and rolling out the disk of dough, turning it often to keep it round. Continue to roll the dough until ⅛ inch thick and about 12 inches in diameter. Gently roll the dough onto the rolling pin. Position the dough over a 9-inch pie plate and carefully unroll the dough into the pan. Using your hands, gently press the dough into the bottom and up the sides of the pan. Tuck the excess dough under itself all around to form a raised edge.

To make a decorative edge on the crust (called "crimping"), use the pointer finger of one hand to press into the raised edge of dough while pinching the dough on either side with the thumb and pointer finger of your other hand. Do this all around the edge of the crust to create a wavy look. Refrigerate the crust for 30 minutes.

Preheat the oven to 350°F.

Line the crust with parchment paper or foil to cover the bottom and sides. Fill the lined crust with pie weights, dried beans, or rice to weight down the dough. Bake for 15 minutes to set the crust. Take the crust out of the oven and set aside to cool slightly, then lift out the foil and pie weights.

Increase the oven temperature to 375°F.

In a large bowl, whisk together the sugar, corn syrup, melted butter, bourbon, and eggs. Stir in the chocolate chips and pecan halves and pieces. Pour the mixture into the crust and place the pie on a baking sheet.

Bake the pie until the top is deep golden brown and the middle is just set, 35 to 40 minutes. Allow the pie to cool completely, at least 1 hour.

MAKE THE BROWN SUGAR CRÈME FRAÎCHE: In a stand mixer fitted with the whisk attachment, whip the crème fraîche, heavy cream, brown sugar, confectioners' sugar, and vanilla on high speed until smooth and fluffy.

Serve the pie warm or at room temperature with the brown sugar crème fraîche.

INSIDER TIP • PIES TO BARS

Most pies can easily be made into bar cookies. Make 1½ times the pie filling. Then make 1½ times the tart dough from Peach and Raspberry Pecan Frangipane Tart (page 178). Line an 11 x 7-inch baking pan with the dough and parbake it at 350°F for about 15 minutes to set it. Then increase the oven temperature to 375°F, top the crust with the pie filling, and bake until set, 35 to 40 minutes.

PEACH AND RASPBERRY PECAN FRANGIPANE TART

MAKES ONE 9-INCH TART

The word "frangipane" is used for a type of nut filling typically used in tarts. This one is a great swap-out recipe. You can change the nuts you use, as well as the fruit. Serve the tart with Raspberry Coulis (page 83).

SPECIAL EQUIPMENT: 9-inch tart pan with a removable bottom

DOUGH
3⅓ cups all-purpose flour
1 cup confectioners' sugar
1¼ teaspoons kosher salt
¾ pound (3 sticks) cold unsalted butter, cubed
3 large eggs

FILLING
1¼ cups pecan halves
½ cup + 3 tablespoons granulated sugar
2 tablespoons all-purpose flour
Pinch of kosher salt

¼ pound (1 stick) + 1 tablespoon unsalted butter, at room temperature
1 large egg
1 large egg white

FRUIT
4 peaches, peeled (see Insider Tip), pitted, and sliced ¼ inch thick
1 pint raspberries
¼ cup granulated sugar
1 tablespoon bourbon

Confectioners' sugar, for sprinkling

MAKE THE DOUGH: In a stand mixer fitted with the paddle attachment, mix together the flour, confectioners' sugar, and salt on low speed. Add the butter and mix until the butter is in pea-size pieces. Beat in the eggs one at a time. Make sure all of the ingredients are evenly combined. Transfer the dough to a covered storage container or wrap in plastic and refrigerate for at least 3 hours before using. (This dough freezes well. I like to roll it out to the size of a baking sheet right after it has been mixed and then freeze it.)

(continued on page 180)

MAKE THE FILLING: In a food processer, combine the pecans and granulated sugar and pulse until the nuts are ground and the mixture resembles coarse cornmeal. Add the flour and salt and pulse twice. Add the butter a bit at a time and pulse until combined. Add the egg and egg white and process until combined. Stop and scrape the bowl; pulse again to make sure everything is smooth and combined. Refrigerate the filling for at least 30 minutes before using.

PREPARE THE FRUIT: In a bowl, toss together the peaches, raspberries, granulated sugar, and bourbon. Set aside to macerate for 10 to 20 minutes.

While the fruit is macerating, preheat the oven to 350°F.

Roll out the dough to a 12-inch round. Gently roll the dough onto the rolling pin. Position the dough over a 9-inch fluted tart pan with a removable bottom and carefully unroll the dough into the pan. Gently press the dough into the bottom and up the sides of the pan. Roll a rolling pin over the sides of the tart pan to cut off the excess dough (save the scraps for another use, if you'd like). Line the tart crust with parchment paper or foil to cover the bottom and sides. Fill the lined crust with pie weights, dried beans, or rice to weight the dough down. Bake for 10 minutes to set the crust. Take the crust out of the oven and set aside to cool slightly, then lift out the foil and pie weights. Leave the oven on.

Spread the filling in the crust. Drain off any excess liquid from the fruit and arrange the fruit on top of the filling. For looks and even baking, I like to lay all of my peach slices down first, followed by the raspberries. Bake the crust until a medium golden brown color, 25 to 35 minutes; rotate the pan front to back halfway through. Transfer the tart to a wire rack to cool completely. Remove the sides of the tart pan. Sprinkle with confectioners' sugar when cooled.

INSIDER TIP • PEELING PEACHES

Bring a large pot of water to a boil. Set up an ice bath (a large bowl with ice and water). With a sharp knife, cut an "X" into the skin on the bottom of each peach. Add the peaches to the boiling water and cook for 1 minute. Transfer the peaches to the ice bath to stop the cooking. Gently peel off the skins, starting at the "X."

Make Your Own

VANILLA EXTRACT

MAKES 1 CUP

This is easy and satisfying, and makes a great gift! There are several choices for the alcohol to use here. Each will yield a different flavor extract, so experiment to find what you like. The rum can be either light or dark.

3 vanilla beans, split lengthwise
1 cup vodka, rum, or bourbon

1 tablespoon water

Scrape the seeds of the vanilla beans and put them and the vanilla bean halves in a 1-pint (16-ounce) jar, bending the beans in half to fit, if necessary. Pour in the liquor and water. Cap the jar tightly and shake it. Refrigerate for 1 month, occasionally shaking the jar to mix it up.

BAKING POWDER

MAKES 6 TABLESPOONS

Baking powder is really just a combination of baking soda and an acid (in this case, cream of tartar) that activates the baking soda when they're combined with a liquid. This homemade version is not what is called "double-acting" (which releases gas first when it gets wet and again in reaction to the heat of the oven) and if you use it, you should be sure to get your batter straight into the oven so that the rising power doesn't dissipate as the batter sits. You can scale this up or down, as long as you keep the 2:1 ratio of cream of tartar to baking soda. Note: You can't make your own baking soda so don't even try it!

¼ cup cream of tartar

2 tablespoons baking soda

Mix the two ingredients together. That's it!

BLACK AND WHITE CRÊPE CAKE

SERVES 8 TO 10

You can decorate the top of this cake with nuts, fresh fruit, or shaved chocolate just before serving. **SPECIAL EQUIPMENT:** 8-inch cake ring (optional), 8-inch round cardboard cake circle, offset spatula

Vanilla Pastry Cream (page 77), cooled
Double recipe Crêpes (page 87)

Chocolate Glaze (page 66), at the temperature of a warm bath

Transfer the pastry cream to a large bowl.

Use an 8-inch cake ring to cut the crêpes; discard the trimmings. (This step is optional—it's just to make the crêpes all the same size, and makes for a nice, neat presentation.)

Place one crêpe on an 8-inch round cardboard cake circle sitting on a wire rack. Spread ⅛ inch of pastry cream evenly over the crêpe. Repeat the process, stacking the crêpes on top of each other. Leave the top crêpe uncovered, with no pastry cream. Refrigerate the cake for at least 2 hours before glazing.

To glaze the cake, pour about 1 cup of the glaze over the top of the stacked crêpes and let it drip down the sides. Pour more glaze as needed to cover the sides of the cake. Refrigerate the cake for at least 1 hour to set the glaze.

Transfer the cake (on the cake board) to a cake plate. Cut into narrow wedges to serve.

INSIDER TIP • CAKE RINGS

A cake ring looks like a cake pan, but it has no bottom. It's just a band of sturdy metal. In the professional kitchen, cakes rings are often used to cut round layers out of cakes that have been baked in large sheet pans.

SUGAR LOLLIPOPS

MAKES ABOUT TWENTY-FOUR 2-INCH LOLLIPOPS

I know lollipops sound juvenile, and you might wonder how they fit in at an upscale restaurant, but there is something so visually stunning about seeing them all bundled together. The bonus here is that lollipops are super easy to make, but you will get the most incredible praise from your guests. **SPECIAL EQUIPMENT:** lollipop molds (optional); lollipop sticks; candy thermometer

Cooking spray, for the mold (if using)
2¼ cups sugar
¾ cup water
⅔ cup light corn syrup
2 drops extract or flavoring of choice
2 drops food coloring of choice

If using a mold, lightly coat it with cooking spray and set aside. If using a nonstick liner, place it on a baking sheet.

In a medium heavy-bottomed saucepan, combine the sugar, water, and corn syrup. Stir over medium heat to dissolve the sugar. Insert a candy thermometer and cook the syrup until it reaches 315°F, what's known as "hard crack" stage (see Glossary, page 192). Take the syrup off the heat. Using a silicone spatula or wooden spoon, stir in the flavoring and coloring.

If using a mold, carefully pour the hot syrup into the mold and insert the lollipop sticks. If using a nonstick liner, carefully pour about 1 tablespoon of the syrup onto the liner and let it settle into a round shape. Place a stick into each pop and rotate the stick, coating it in the syrup for a better hold. Let the lollipops cool about 1 hour before serving.

chef it up!

If you're making these pops for grown-ups, think about some of your favorite cocktails for inspiration. I once made mojito lollipops, adding 2 drops mint extract, 1 tablespoon lime juice, and 1 tablespoon white rum.

CHOCOLATE-DIPPED MARSHMALLOWS

MAKES ABOUT 16 MARSHMALLOWS

As a kid, I remember my mom would buy us these little chocolate-covered marshmallow twists from the kosher store down the street. I loved them so much and was hooked at first bite. Soon after, everyone in my family started buying me marshmallow-related treats. The ever-popular Peeps, chocolate-covered marshmallow Santas, and Mallomars were among my favorites. Using this base marshmallow recipe, the possibilities of flavoring and toppings are endless. One of my personal favorites is chocolate-dipped mint marshmallows topped with crushed candy canes. Really great for holiday gift giving! **SPECIAL EQUIPMENT:** candy thermometer

NONSTICK MIX
1 cup confectioners' sugar
½ cup cornstarch

MARSHMALLOWS
Cooking spray, for greasing the pan
1 envelope (¼ ounce) unflavored
   powdered gelatin (2½ teaspoons)
½ cup water
1 cup granulated sugar

½ cup light corn syrup
1 teaspoon vanilla extract
Pinch of kosher salt

DIP AND TOPPING
1½ cups semisweet chocolate chips
2 teaspoons canola oil
1 cup chopped nuts, crushed candy
   (such as candy canes), sprinkles, or
   crushed cookies

MAKE THE NONSTICK MIX: Sift the confectioners' sugar and cornstarch together into a small bowl and set aside.

MAKE THE MARSHMALLOWS: Coat an 8-inch square baking pan with cooking spray.

In a small microwave-safe bowl, sprinkle the gelatin over ¼ cup of the water

(continued on page 188)

and set aside to soften for about 5 minutes. Put the bowl in the microwave and cook on high for 20 seconds to melt the gelatin. Set aside.

In a small, heavy-bottomed saucepan, combine the granulated sugar, remaining ¼ cup water, and ¼ cup of the corn syrup. Cook over high heat until it reaches 238°F on a candy thermometer.

While the sugar mixture is cooking, in a stand mixer fitted with the whisk attachment, whisk the remaining ¼ cup corn syrup on low speed. Pour in the melted gelatin and continue to whip.

When the sugar syrup has reached 238°F, with the mixer running, slowly pour the hot syrup down along the side of the bowl. Don't dump in the syrup quickly, as it might hit the whisk and splatter you in the face; this can burn you very badly—not fun. Slow and steady wins on this one. Once all of the syrup has been added, turn up the speed to medium-high and whip until it comes about three-quarters of the way up the sides and looks opaque, about 7 minutes. Beat in the vanilla and salt. Whip for 1 minute to combine evenly.

Pour the mixture out into the prepared pan and spread it evenly with a rubber spatula. Sift the nonstick mix over the top and let set at room temperature, uncovered, for at least 5 hours.

Invert out onto a cutting board and cut the marshmallows into your desired shape. (I generally prefer rectangles.) If they begin to stick to your knife while cutting, dip your knife into the nonstick mix.

MAKE THE DIP: In a heavy-bottomed saucepan or in the microwave, melt the chocolate chips. Mix in the canola oil and pour into a narrow, deep bowl.

Line a baking sheet with parchment paper or set a wire cooling rack over a piece of parchment paper. One at a time, dip the marshmallows in the chocolate to coat them and place on the baking sheet or wire rack. Before the chocolate has cooled completely, sprinkle with your topping of choice. Just before they are completely set, move them to a different spot to eliminate "feet" forming on the bottoms from the chocolate that has run off. Allow chocolate to completely set and cool. Store airtight at room temperature.

chef it up! MAKE YOUR OWN MARSHMALLOW CHICKS

Line a baking sheet with a silicone liner. Make the marshmallow mixture as directed, adding a couple of drops of food coloring to get the color of chick you want. Take the recipe up to the point of beating in the vanilla and salt.

At this point, instead of spreading the marshmallow mixture in a pan, you're going to pipe little chicks. Fill a pastry bag fitted with a #9 plain tip. Hold the decorating tip an inch above the silicone liner, at a 90-degree angle, and pipe out a 1-inch mound of marshmallow. With the tip still connected to the marshmallow (but with you no longer squeezing any out), pull the mound out on one side into a teardrop shape, and at the same time pull up to make the chick's tail. Then, at the head end, pipe a smaller mound and pull it toward the tail and then switch back the other way to make the beak. Make all of the chicks and let them sit about 5 minutes.

In a large bowl, whisk a couple of drops of food coloring into granulated sugar (which will be used for coating the chicks). Toss the chicks gently in the sugar to coat them. Let them chill out and dry.

appendix

GLOSSARY

Throughout this book and in the world of baking, you will come across terms that are unfamiliar and may sound intimidating. Here is a glossary of some that you should know in order to perfect your baking knowledge.

BLOOM: In the baking world, bloom has two definitions. 1) To "bloom gelatin" is to rehydrate it in water to soften it and make it useable. 2) "Bloom" also refers to the white spots sometimes seen on chocolate. The bloom is actually the whitish cocoa butter or sugar in the chocolate separating itself from the cocoa mass.

CARAMELIZE: To heat sugar (or a substance that contains sugar) until it turns brown

CORNET: A small paper cone used for writing and making small line decorations on cakes and other baked goods with icing (see "Decorating with Icing," page 73)

CREAM (VERB): To mix sugar and butter together to incorporate air into them. This results in a lighter texture in baked goods. You will often see instructions in a recipe to "cream butter and sugar until light and fluffy." It's important to stop when you've reached the fluffy stage, because if you continue beating, the mixture will lose the air bubbles and the purpose will be defeated.

CRYSTALLIZATION: When sugar and water are melted together over heat to make a syrup, there is a limit to how much sugar can be dissolved. When the syrup reaches that limit, it is said to be saturated. If the syrup goes beyond the saturation point, the excess sugar un-dissolves and reverts to a crystalline form. A syrup that has "crystallized" will make whatever candy (or other mixture) it is used in grainy.

CUT IN: This is a method for adding cold butter or other solid fat to flour. It's done by hand with your fingers, with a pastry blender, or by using two knives (used like scissors, cross-cutting the fat into the flour). The end result is a shaggy dough with pea-size pieces of fat dispersed throughout. You'll see this method called for in making pie crusts and sometimes scones.

EGG WASH: A mixture of eggs with either milk or water, used to brush on un-cooked dough before baking. The wash creates a sheen and golden brown color. A typical egg wash is 2 eggs whisked with 1 tablespoon water or milk.

GLUTEN: This is a protein found in wheat flour. To activate the gluten, liquid is added to flour to form a dough (as for bread) and the dough is then kneaded. The kneading action develops the gluten, giving the dough structure and stretch. The more you knead, the more the gluten is developed.

ICE BATH: A bowl of cold water and ice, used to cool down hot liquids. The bowl containing the hot liquid is set directly into the ice bath.

MEDIUM PEAKS: A stage of whipping between soft peaks and stiff peaks (see below)

NAPPÉ: A French term that describes the stage in which a sauce has thickened enough to "coat the back of a spoon"

PROOF: Proof has two meanings in baking. The first is the process of testing to see if the yeast you are using is still active: Sprinkle it over warm (105° to 110°F) water, usually with a pinch of sugar, to see if the yeast starts to bubble. This is the "proof" that the yeast is alive and well. But in professional bak-ing, the word "proof" also means to let a yeast-based dough rest and grow in size (home cooks usually call this "letting the dough rise"). Proofing is ideally done in an environment of 90° to 100°F. Always cover the dough to be proofed. Tip: Preheat your oven to 350°F, shut it off, then stick the dough that needs to rise in the oven and leave the oven door open.

RIBBON STAGE: This describes when egg yolks, or a combination of yolks and sugar, have reached their full volume potential through whipping. You know this has been achieved when the whisk is lifted in the air and the mixture falls back into the bowl, creating a ribbon that loops back on top of itself.

SIFT: To pass dry ingredients through a sieve, sifter, or other fine screen. There are two main reasons for sifting: 1) To evenly mix a group of dry ingredients, such as baking powder and soda, with flour, and 2) to eliminate any clumps or lumps in the dry ingredient(s).

SIMPLE SYRUP: A liquid made by dissolving sugar in water over heat. It's always a 1:1 ratio of water to sugar. It's useful for many dessert applications and should be in every pastry chef's repertoire. Simple syrup will keep in the refrigerator for up to 1 month.

SOFT PEAKS: A stage reached by beaten egg whites or cream. To test, lift the whisk or beater out of the mixture; the whipped substance holds a peak that just barely stands and then falls to the side.

STIFF PEAKS: A stage reached by beaten egg whites or cream. To test, lift the whisk or beater out of the mixture; the whipped substance forms a peak that stands straight up.

SUGAR STAGES: When you cook sugar and water, the water evaporates and the sugar slowly cooks to different stages with different properties. The most common sugar stages used in baking are soft ball, hard crack, and caramel. These stages describe how the sugar will set after it has been cooked. In this book, I use the soft ball stage to make buttercream frostings and fudge; hard crack stage is used to make Sugar Lollipops (page 184); and sugar is taken to the caramel stage for the Chocolate-Caramel Hot Cocoa Mix (page 117). The best way to monitor this is with a candy thermometer, but there are also visual tests that the cook can use.

• Soft Ball: 238° to 240°F. Tested by dropping a small amount of the hot syrup into cold water. It should hold the shape of a ball and be pliable and soft, hence soft ball.

• Hard Crack: 300° to 310°F. Tested by dropping a small amount of the hot syrup onto a plate. It should quickly set up hard and will crack.

• Caramel: 320° to 348°F. The sugar will turn a golden brown color.

TEMPER (VERB): What you do when you have to combine two substances of different temperatures. The most common situation is when you have to add hot milk to cold eggs. After the milk is heated, you slowly add some of it to the cold eggs while constantly whisking, bringing the eggs closer to the temperature of the milk. Then the mixture can be added back to the remaining hot milk. (If you add the hot milk to the eggs too rapidly, they will cook and be unusable in your recipe.)

WATER BATH: Some baked custards (like the cheesecakes in this book) and puddings require moist, gentle heat to prevent them from cracking. A water bath is a deep pan filled halfway with water that heats in the oven and creates both steam and a more gentle, even heat. Here are some tips for a successful water bath.

• If making something in a springform pan (like cheesecake), make sure to wrap the outside of the pan tightly with foil to seal off the seams of the springform pan. This keeps water from getting into the pan.

• Place the custard, cheesecake, or pudding in a roasting pan big enough to hold the pan (or custard cups) comfortably. Place the roasting pan on a pulled-out oven rack. Fill the roasting pan with hot water to come halfway up the sides of whatever you are baking. Then carefully slide the oven rack in.

• Let cheesecake cool completely in the water bath before removing it. But take out custards and puddings to cool.

ZEST: The very thin colored outer layer of citrus peels. The spongy white underneath of the peel, known as the pith, is often bitter and unappetizing, so be careful to only use the zest of the fruit when called for.

INGREDIENTS & SUBSTITUTIONS

ALL-PURPOSE FLOUR: Comes either bleached or unbleached. Flours are usually defined by their protein (gluten) content: high protein for baked goods that need structure (like bread) and low protein for items like cake, where you want the baked good to be tender. All-purpose flour is in the middle with a protein level that is neither high nor low.

BAKING POWDER: A chemical leavener made up of a combination of a weak acid and an alkaline substance (baking soda). When liquid is added, the acid and alkaline substances interact and produce carbon dioxide gas, which leavens the baked good. **SUBSTITUTION:** If you're a DIY kind of person, you can make your own; see page 181.

BAKING SODA: A chemical leavener that reacts with acid to form carbon dioxide for added lift and a lighter texture

BROWN SUGAR: Granulated sugar with the addition of molasses. **SUBSTITUTION:** If you are out of brown sugar but happen to have molasses (not blackstrap) and regular sugar on hand, here's a way to make your own brown sugar: For every 1 cup of granulated white sugar, blend in 1½ tablespoons molasses in a food processor, or in a bowl with a fork.

BUTTER: With rare exceptions (which are noted), all my recipes call for unsalted butter. **SUBSTITUTION:** If you only have salted on hand, use it but omit any salt added to the recipe. You cannot substitute butter spreads for real butter. Spreads contain more water and will make your cookies or cake . . . well . . . spread too much.

BUTTERMILK: With its viscosity and acidity, buttermilk improves the texture of baked goods. The acid in buttermilk reacts with baking soda to create carbon dioxide and leaven batters. Buttermilk also helps fight oxidation of any fruit in a recipe. **SUBSTITUTION:** If you don't have buttermilk, you can easily make your own, using whole milk or heavy cream: For every 1 cup of milk or cream, stir in 1 tablespoon lemon juice. Let stand for 10 minutes at room temperature before using. (It will curdle slightly, but that's what it's supposed to do.)

CAKE FLOUR: Bleached wheat flour with one of the lowest protein contents, this gives baked goods a more tender texture. Be sure not to confuse this with self-rising flour, which has leavening agents and salt already in it.

CHOCOLATE: Comes in varying ratios of cocoa butter to cocoa solids and can include sugar and dairy. The chocolate with the most cocoa solids and the least cocoa butter and dairy is dark chocolate. On the other end of the spectrum is white chocolate. Right in the middle is milk chocolate.

COCOA POWDER: I usually use Dutch-process cocoa powder, which has a slightly milder flavor than regular (natural) cocoa. Cocoa powder that has been Dutched has been treated with an alkalizing agent to reduce the cocoa's natural acidity. But for all the recipes in this book, I used regular cocoa powder. Use whichever you prefer or have on hand.

CONFECTIONERS' SUGAR: In the professional baking world, this is referred to as 10X sugar, which means that it's granulated sugar ground 10 times to a fine powder. It is then combined with a little cornstarch to prevent clumps.

CORN SYRUP: A sweet syrup made from corn, often used in the world of pastry to prevent sugar crystallization

CORNSTARCH: A thickener used in puddings or other fillings. **SUBSTITUTION:** For thickening, you can substitute 2 tablespoons all-purpose flour for every 1 tablespoon cornstarch called for.

CRÈME FRAÎCHE: Similar to sour cream but milder, with a higher fat content **SUBSTITUTION:** If a recipe calls for crème fraîche and your store doesn't carry it, or you want to bake something spur of the moment and don't have any on hand, you can use the same amount of sour cream or Greek yogurt. (The reverse is also true: you can swap in an equal measure of crème fraîche for sour cream or Greek yogurt.)

GELATIN: A substance often made from animal collagen, used as a gelling agent. Gelatin can be purchased in two forms: sheets and powdered. A sheet of gelatin is the equivalent of about 1 teaspoon of the powdered. An envelope of powdered gelatin contains 2½ teaspoons and will usually gel 2 cups of liquid. Both forms of gelatin need to be softened in water before using in a recipe.

GLUCOSE: A form of sugar that is absorbed directly into the bloodstream. Glucose is used in baking to help stop the crystallization of sugar and improve texture.

GRAPESEED OIL: An oil extracted from grape seeds; used in cooking because of its subtle taste and high smoke point

MILK, CONDENSED: Whole milk that has had most of the water removed and sugar added

MILK, EVAPORATED: Milk that has had a little less than half of its water removed. You can get it in whole, low-fat, and fat-free forms. **SUBSTITUTION:** You can use whole milk for evaporated milk and vice versa.

SHORTENING: A hydrogenated vegetable oil that is solid at room temperature

VANILLA BEAN: A pod harvested from an orchid plant, used as a flavoring. There is no substitution for the intense flavor that you get from vanilla seeds, so I almost always opt for them. It's definitely worth the investment if you plan on doing any serious baking or dessert making, although I find that a good alternative is to use vanilla paste (see Insider Tip, page 40).

VANILLA EXTRACT: A flavoring made by the aging vanilla beans in a mixture of alcohol and water. You can actually make your own; see page 181.

YEAST: A natural fungus used as a leavening agent in baked goods. In the restaurant world, it's more common to use what is known as "cake yeast" or "fresh yeast." Unfortunately, cake yeast is not always easy to find in super-markets—as opposed to active dry yeast, which can be found everywhere. Active dry yeast needs to be rehydrated to activate; that's why yeast recipes commonly call for you to combine the yeast with warm water or milk first. Yeast is a living organism that needs to eat. And what does yeast like to eat? Sugar. Not a bad diet. As the yeast eats the sugar, it releases carbon dioxide into the dough, causing it to rise.

EQUIPMENT

ANGEL FOOD CAKE PAN: This is a tube pan with little extensions on its rim so that when you cool the cake upside down, the pan can rest on them and the air can circulate better around the pan. You can make an angel food cake in a regular tube pan and cool the cake upside down by hanging it on a bottle (see page 24).

BAKING PANS: In general, anything baked in a dark baking pan (as opposed to the light-colored aluminum pans) will bake faster. If using dark pans, drop the oven temperature down by 15°F or cut the baking time down by 5 to 10 minutes. If using glass pans, you'll have to add baking time. In general, it's wise to check your baked items in the oven sooner than later.

BAKING SHEETS: Home-style baking sheets come in lots of different sizes (as opposed to restaurant baking sheets, which are pretty standardized). They can have no sides (cookie sheets) or have a rim that runs around the outside, usually about 1 inch deep. In this book, if the rimmed type of pan is needed, the recipe will say so.

BENCH SCRAPER: A flat metal rectangle with a handle, a bench scraper is a tool used in baking to gently lift stuck dough off a surface. It also aids in cleanup when you need to "scrape" bits and pieces of food left behind on your work surface. Bench scrapers are also useful for gathering up and transporting small cut-up foods from a cutting board to a bowl.

CAKE BOARDS: Cardboard rounds used to support the bottom of a cake, typically the same diameter as the cake. Cake boards can be found in most craft and baking supply stores, or you can make your own by cutting out a round of sturdy cardboard.

CAKE PANS: Cake pans come in many sizes, but the important thing for the recipes in this book is that they be 2 inches deep. Note that if your pans are "nonstick," you still need to grease them or line them (depending on what the recipe calls for), because nonstick does not stay nonstick for very long. See also "Baking pans," above.

CAKE RINGS: Stainless steel rings, found in various diameters, for cutting cake layers and building layered desserts. Unlike a cake pan, a cake ring has no bottom. When used for building layered desserts, there needs to be a cake board placed on the bottom. Cake rings are mostly found in specialty kitchen or baking supply stores.

CANNELLE MOLDS: Small fluted cuplike molds, deeper than they are wide. They come in a range of sizes, with the biggest being a little over 2 inches. They are used to make a French pastry called *cannelé*. I prefer copper molds because they conduct heat well to create a better crust; the copper also "seasons" as you use them, creating an almost nonstick surface. You can also buy trays of silicone molds, which are less expensive, but they won't give the pastries the same thick, dark crust—though the results will be just as delicious.

COOKIE SCOOPS: Like ice cream scoops, but smaller. Used to perfectly and consistently portion dough. They come in a range of sizes, from in the neighborhood of 1 tablespoon to ¼ cup.

DOUBLE BOILER: There are two-part pots that are sold as double boilers, and some saucepans are sold with a double boiler insert. But in a restaurant kitchen, we always just make our own double boilers with a bowl set over a pot of simmering water. The heat and steam from the water heats the bottom of the bowl, melting or gently cooking whatever is in the bowl. When setting up a double boiler, make sure the bowl is the same diameter as or bigger than the top of the pot. Never choose a bowl that sits directly in the water, or else you run the risk of burning your food. And, of course, the bowl should be heatproof; a stainless steel bowl is ideal.

DOUGH HOOK: The hook attachment for the stand mixer is used to make dough, mostly bread. Its unique shape mechanically kneads the dough to develop the gluten that gives the baked good its structure.

NONSTICK SILICONE LINER: I find this item to be indispensable in my kitchen, not only for baking but to use when rolling out dough on the counter. It works much the same as parchment paper, but can be washed and reused many times. Silpat is one brand name of nonstick liner.

OFFSET SPATULA: A metal spatula whose blade is bent, i.e., not in a straight line with the handle. Large offset spatulas are used for moving baked goods from one place to another. Small spatulas are used for frosting and decorating cakes.

PADDLE ATTACHMENT: Also known as the beater, this is the flat metal attachment for the stand mixer, mostly used for creaming ingredients.

PARCHMENT PAPER: Baking-grade paper made for high heat. To make the paper nonstick, it is coated with silicone.

PASTRY BAGS: Cone-shaped bags of either disposable plastic or reusable cloth, used for piping dough or decorating pastries. See "Decorating with Icing," page 73.

PASTRY BRUSHES: A kitchen-grade bristle brush, used for applying egg wash or melted butter to the top of dough, removing excess flour, and other pastry applications

PASTRY TIPS: Metal tips that fit into pastry bags, for piping dough and decorating. There are tons of different styles of pastry tips, but the two that are used the most in a restaurant kitchen are the plain (aka straight) tip and the star tip, in a variety of sizes. See "Decorating with Icing," page 73.

PIZZELLE IRON: Similar to a waffle iron, but with a round, more shallow etched pattern. Used to make thin Italian-style cookies of the same name.

ROLLING PINS: Although any sort of rolling pin gets the job done, I like to use a French-style rolling pin for rolling out dough. It is a single piece of wood with tapered ends, not handles. Using this type of pin gives me much more control over the rolling process.

SPIDER: A long-handled wire-mesh or slotted tool, typically used to lift food out of hot oil or boiling water

SPRINGFORM PAN: A pan with a removable bottom and pan sides that are released by undoing its clamp-style closure. Used for wet cakes, like cheesecake, that you wouldn't, or couldn't, invert out of a pan.

STAND MIXER: A countertop mixer that usually has a strong motor (as opposed to hand mixers). Typically comes with different mixing attachments. See whisk attachment, paddle attachment, and dough hook.

THERMOMETERS: The most important thermometer to have for this book is one that can read up to 400°F, for candy making and deep-frying. The same thermometer can be used for either operation. In fact, such thermometers are often sold as dual-purpose tools.

WHISK ATTACHMENT: Also known as the whip, a wire attachment for a stand mixer, used to incorporate air into ingredients.

ZESTER: The best tool for grating the zest of citrus fruits is a rasp-style Microplane zester/grater. Microplanes are really sharp, and it's easy to be sure that you only get the flavorful zest (the colored outer layer).

ACKNOWLEDGMENTS

This book would not have been possible if it weren't for the love and support of my family and friends.

To my husband Ted "you know what . . . ." Thank you for being my best friend, my love, support, and my biggest fan.

To my little sous-chef, my "Buggy" Dean. You are truly a blessing and I enjoy every moment of watching you grow up. Mommy loves you more than words can say.

Huge thanks to Rachael Ray for believing in me and helping to make my dreams come true. You are an inspiration and I am truly grateful.

Last but not least, to Ro. You're the master at keeping it all together; I don't know how you do it. Thank you for the countless hours of work, all the runs to the grocery store, and seemingly endless bowls of pasta!

index